# Golf Stole My Brain

# Golf Stole My Brain

## AND OTHER STRANGE GOLFING TALES

### DALE CONCANNON

metro

First published by Metro Publishing,
an imprint of
John Blake Publishing Limited
3 Bramber Court, 2 Bramber Road
London W14 9PB

www.johnblakepublishing.co.uk

www.facebook.com/johnblakebooks ■
twitter.com/jblakebooks ■

First published in hardback in 2015

ISBN: 978-1-78418-769-9

British Library Cataloguing-in-Publication Data:

A catalogue record for this book is available from the British Library.

Design by www.envydesign.co.uk

Printed in Great Britain by CPI Group (UK) Ltd

1 3 5 7 9 10 8 6 4 2

Papers used by John Blake Publishing are natural, recyclable products made from
wood grown in sustainable forests. The manufacturing processes conform to the
environmental regulations of the country of origin.

Every attempt has been made to contact the relevant copyright-holders, but some
were unobtainable. We would be grateful if the appropriate people could contact us.

# Acknowledgements

_T_his book is dedicated to my two godchildren, Jack William Groom and Elle Davis Groom.

The author would like to extend his sincere and grateful thanks to the following people:

David Cronin; Dave Musgrove; Laura Concannon; Roddy Carr; Timothy Ward; Mark Roe; Andrew Coltart; Thomas Bjørn; Hugh Grant; Robert Aziz; Graham Rowley of Old Sport Auctions; John Sinnott; John McSharry; Bob Zafian and Ryan Carey of Green Jacket Auctions; Mizuno; Matthew Harris of the Golf Picture Library; Callaway; Steve Beddow; Getty Images; Old Golf Images; D. J. Russell; Ronan Rafferty; Peter Oosterhuis; John Jacobs; Warren Humphreys; Rick and Sue Cressman of Nailcote Hall; Andy Prodger; Bernhard

Langer; Renton Laidlaw; Ian Woosnam; William and Rose Rinn; Tony Jacklin; Frank Christian; Archie Baird of the Gullane Golf Museum; Peter Baker; Scott Crockett; Bob Warters; Archerfield Links; Leah Rinn; Golf Images; Yvette Groom; Bespoke Golf Images & Interiors (UK); Pete Masters; *Golf World;* Jock Howard; PGA European Tour Media Department; NASA Space Center, Houston, TX; Turkish Airlines; La Jenny Resort (France); Michele Mair of IMG; Ian Connelly; Peter Entwistle; Ron Halley; Walter Mechilli.

Finally a huge thank you to Toby Buchan, Executive Editor of John Blake Publishing Limited, for his unfailing politeness and dedication in getting this book published. The same applies to his highly professional design team who also did such a great job.

Other photograph credits:
Page 26, © Chris Graythen/Getty Images; page 53, © Gordon Priestley/*Daily Mail*/REX Shutterstock; page 83, © Warren Little/Getty Images; page 92, © Scott Halleran/ Getty Images; page 103, © *Boston Globe*/Getty Images; page 144, © Phil Sheldon/Popperfoto/Getty Images; page 145, © Mike Ehrmann/Getty Images; page 183, © Robyn Beck/AFP/Getty Images.

# Author's Note

The story of golf is full of wacky individuals who obsess over a missed putt or wayward drive. From the player who bet his life on a round of golf, to the complete novice who fancied he could take on the world's best players in the Open Golf Championship, this book reveals some of the best and worst golfers ever to pick up a titanium three wood! The product of many years' research, it contains a mass of little-known and hitherto unpublished stories (for the title story, see page 29). The same applies to the photography. Illustrated throughout with some of the most unusual photographs ever taken, it's entertaining, informative but above all fun. So take a look – perhaps you may even recognise someone you know!

DALE CONCANNON

## SCARFACE SHANKS SHOT

**Alphonse 'Al' Capone** accidentally shot himself in 1928 after a game of golf with gang member Johnny Patton. The notorious gangster was getting into a car in the parking lot of the Burnham Woods golf course near Chicago on 15 September when his .45 pistol discharged in his right trouser pocket, the bullet passing through both his legs. 'Scarface' was rushed to St Margaret's Hospital in the Hammond area of the city. Afraid his weakened condition might lead to an attack by a rival gang, he registered under the name of Geary. In hospital for three days, his entourage occupied five rooms with gun-carrying hoodlums on guard twenty-four hours a day. He made a full recovery but it was not the only on-course accidental shooting he suffered from. Three years earlier, he was rifling through his golf bag when a pistol without the safety on shot him through the foot.

## AUSSIE RULED

An **Australian** golfer visited Ceylon in 1926 and defeated every player of note until somebody mentioned a mysterious caddie who played with just two clubs – a driver and a mid-iron. Told he was practically unbeatable, the club pro at Colombo confirmed the story adding that the caddie had never taken more than one putt on any green five times in the past year! The caddie, always dressed in a conventional batik skirt, had a peculiar flat-footed stance but his body acted like a steel spring and he hit the longest ball ever seen. Intrigued, the Australian challenged the unnamed caddie by telegraph and he paid for him to board the next train to Nuwara Eliya for the match. Travelling all night in a third-class compartment without getting a wink of sleep, the caddie turned up on the first tee the next day with his two clubs. Barely uttering a sound he gave the Australian the beating of his life. Picking up his fee without saying a word, he returned to Colombo and was never heard of again.

## TEN THOUSAND-TO-ONE ODDS-ON FAVOURITE

George Neil, club professional at the Lake Shore Country Club in California, was offered a unique challenge by Chicago lawyer **Alfred S. Austrian**. In 1929, he offered to pay the massive sum of $10,000 if Neil taught him well enough to break 80! No other fees would be paid and both men set about weeks of strenuous toil until the fateful day

when teacher told his pupil, 'Go out and play, then return and pay!' Picking up his clubs Mr Austrian went out three times and scored 78, 79, and 77. As Neil pocketed the cheque, he could not resist asking why his pupil had wanted to break 80 in the first place... Mr Austrian replied, 'To win a $1 bet!'

## A REAL HEADACHE

Known for his repertoire of amazing trick-shots, British professional George **Ashdown** played a full round at Esher Golf Club near London in 1931 striking every shot - including putts - directly off the forehead of his trusting assistant Ena Shaw. Not the first time they had pulled off this unusual trick, she had a rubber tee strapped to her forehead and was required to lie flat on the ground and remain very, very still!

## MASTERFUL INEPTITUDE

**Augusta National Golf Club**, home of the Masters, came close to bankruptcy in December 1935 and was only saved by some smart financial manoeuvring. Hard to imagine today, a letter was sent by its legal representatives to creditors announcing the foreclosure sale of the Fruitland Manor Corporation, which owned the now iconic golf course. Formed by Bobby Jones and Clifford Roberts in 1931, the course and clubhouse were listed as its primary assets. Due to the Great Depression, the new company could not meet its financial obligations, made worse no doubt by hosting the 1934 and 1935 Masters Tournaments (the prize fund

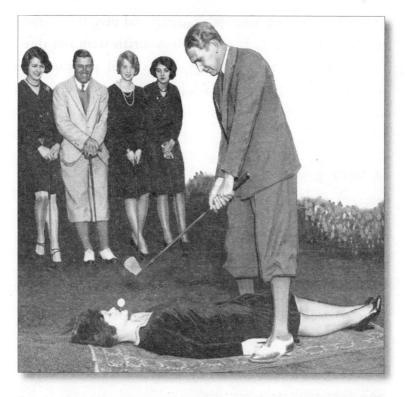

for the second year was $5,000). It was the Fruitland Manor Corporation that went through foreclosure. The land, however, which now contained the Augusta National golf course, was purchased at the foreclosure sale to ensure the survival of the course and Augusta National Golf Club, and a new entity was formed – The Augusta National, Inc. A letter was sent to the creditors from the company attorney offering them a one-time option (to expire three weeks later) to accept Class B stock in The Augusta National, Inc. or to forever relinquish any right as creditor (due to the foreclosure).

## LOSING YOUR HEAD OVER GOLF!

**Amir Abbas Hoveyda**, Prime Minister of Iran, proudly opened a new 18-hole golf course in Tehran in October 1970. A spectacular complex built near the Royal Tehran Hilton Hotel and overlooking the city, the Imperial Country Club was seen as part of Iran's attempt to become more westernised. Sadly it was fairly short-lived. After the 1979 Islamic Revolution, golf was demonised and the Imperial Country Club went quickly downhill. Without water it simply turned to dust, with five holes taken over as a training area by the Revolutionary Guards. Worse still, Prime Minister Hoveyda, who had backed the scheme, was later executed for his 'pro-Western' sympathies.

## LIGHT ON HIS FEET

Hollywood legend Fred **Astaire** completed one of the great golf scenes in movie history in 1937 for his latest RKO. screen musical, *Carefree*. Released in American theatres in October, the 10 handicap star hit a series of teed-up golf balls while dancing around them. Executed to the Irving Berlin song 'Since They Turned Loch Lomond into Swing,' the complex routine took many days of rehearsal to perfect. Although there are only sixteen golf shots used in the movie, Astaire practised eight hours a day for over a week. The actual shooting required two-and-a-half days. The routine was set on the first tee at an exclusive American country club.

## ACES HIGH

The legendary **Arnold Palmer** became the only pro golfer ever to ace the same hole on consecutive days! Playing the 182-yard 3rd hole at the TPC at Avenel, Potomac, Maryland, on 2 September 1986, Palmer holed out using a five-iron in the first round. The next day a local TV news crew showed up at the tee telling him how they were there to film him getting another one! Palmer smiled and told them, 'You're a day late.' He then holed out for a second time! The same crew turned up the following day looking for a three-peat but Arnie missed the green.

## SPACED OUT

Astronaut **Alan B. Shepard Jnr.** became the only man in history to play golf on the moon on 6 February, 1971. Using a modified Wilson six-iron smuggled onto the lunar module, he surprised NASA officials by pulling out two golf balls on the final day of the Apollo 14 mission. 'In my left hand, I have a little white pellet that's familiar to millions of Americans,' he said. 'I'll

drop it down. Unfortunately, the suit is so stiff, I can't do this with two hands, but I'm going to try a little sand-trap shot here…' Hitting them one-handed the first was a straight shank. The other was hit smoothly and according to Shepard travelled: 'miles and miles and miles.' (He later amended this to between 200 and 400 yards in the one-sixth gravity of the moon.) In response, a cable was sent from the R&A stating: 'Please refer to rules of golf on etiquette, paragraph 6… Before leaving a bunker, a player should carefully fill up all holes made by him therein.'

## GOD MUST BE A GOLFER!

Gus **Andreone** is officially the oldest golfer ever to record a hole-in-one after the 103-year old former pro made the eighth ace of his career on 18 December 2014, using a driver on a 113-yard hole at Palm Aire Country Club in Florida. The previous record was held by Elsie McLean, who was 102 when she holed her tee shot in 2007. 'Miracles do happen once in a while,' the 75-year United States PGA member told the Association's website.

## DRIVING AMBITION

Talk about an overriding obsession. A man pleaded guilty to four counts of **bank robbery** in May 2006. At his trial the Maryland resident told police that he needed the money to play golf! Netting a total of $20,896, at least he can afford a few lessons when he gets out in about twenty years time…

## A LATE ENTRY!

A curious incident took place before the British Open began at St Andrews in 1891. David **Brown**, the 1886 champion, had left his entry with Jim Morris in St Andrews a week earlier before returning to North Berwick to practice. Upon his return he discovered that his entry had not been made, so that he could not compete. Completely undaunted, he stood on the first tee until every man had driven and got each one to sign a paper to the effect that if he, Brown, made the lowest score, he should be entitled to the Open title! Playing unofficially he did not win but did finish sixth. Not surprisingly he was told by the committee that there was no prize for him, whereupon a move was made to get up a purse to defray his expenses. Davy, characteristically, declared he was not an object of charity and refused the money. He then challenged the new champion, Hugh Kirkaldy, in a match scheduled the day after the Championship ended. It was a match he won easily by 4 and 3.

## BANJO NEARLY BANJAXED

**Burnham Woods** Golf Club near Chicago opened for play in early 1925. Famous for its connection with legendary mobster Al Capone, rumours persist that it was the burial ground for many of the weapons used in the St Valentine's Day Massacre in 1929. A favourite haunt of Capone, his playing partners included colourfully named characters like Jack (Machine Gun) McGurn, Murray (The Camel) Humphreys, Jake (Greasy Thumb) Guzik, Frederick (Killer) Burke, (Three-Finger) Jack White and Sam (Golf Bag) Hunt. A keen golfer, 'Scarface' would play at least twice a week usually for $500 a hole with side bets totalling many thousands. Al was always surrounded by a dozen or more bodyguards but this did not stop one famous on-course altercation after Capone was accused of cheating by a hoodlum named Banjo Eyes. Pulling a .45 revolver from his golf bag, Al shouted: 'On your knees and start praying.' Known for his violent temper he had to be physically restrained by his men who managed to avoid a very public fairway execution. Then, just as quickly, Capone's black mood turned full circle. Slapping Banjo on the back he acted as if nothing had happened. 'Come on,' he said smiling. 'Let's finish the game!'

## A GOOD WALK SPOILT?

Arthur **Balfour** took part in an unusual debate at the London School of Economics on 14 May 1925. Opposing the former British Prime Minister was Leo Maxse, editor of the *National Review* magazine. One of a series of high-profile debates in aid of King Edward's Hospital Fund, the subject was: 'Does Golf do more Harm than Good?' Presided over by Sir Robert Hudson, the often heated debate took place in front of a large audience. Arguing against golf, Maxse suggested the game was only suitable for keeping middle-aged men out of mischief! 'It diverts politicians from politics,' he said, 'journalists from journalism and takes international financiers, mugwumps, mandarins, bureaucrats, and highbrows away from the various forms of mischief in which they specialise…' He went on to to argue that golf was invented by the Germans about 1410

RT HON

A.J.BALFOUR

"The Pearl Series"

before being 'dumped' on Holland by Teutonic Knights who felt it was no longer a 'suitable game for men of blood and iron…' Balfour counter-argued saying that golf was a 'model of a game which gave healthful satisfaction'. Denying that his recent trip to Palestine was a precursor to turning the Holy Land into a 'gigantic golf links' he did take credit for 'the spread of golf in this country thirty-odd years ago'. He contrasted the fate of the man taken to the seaside by his wife and children with no means of filling the weary hours of leisure, with that of a 'man transported to a healthy climate and beautiful scenery, participating in a game which would exercise all his skill to play even moderately…' He finished by saying how the blessings of golf had been immense and the 'mere fact that some classes to which Mr Maxse has a strong objection get a good deal of pleasure out of the game, is not a sufficient reason for condemning it.'

## GET A GRIP

Which grip do you use – overlapping Vardon grip or interlocking? Two caddies employed at **Belton Park golf course** in Grantham, Lincolnshire, discussed the way a proper player should grip the club. It ended in a fight at the rear of the clubhouse on Sunday, 26 June 1932. Richard John Smith, 21, was struck on the head with an iron club before collapsing on the ground. Taken to the local infirmary he died a short while later. His killer Michael Rouse pleaded guilty to manslaughter but while accepting his argument that the Vardon grip was perhaps better for most golfers the judge still sentenced him to ten years' penal servitude.

## MY BRAIN HURTS

An innovative report in 2008 revealed that when the golfer feels the actual strike of ball on clubface, the ball is already 14 inches down the fairway! It seems the **brain** cannot process information fast enough from the hands when the ball makes impact with the driver. The time lapse isn't quite as long for the average woman golfer, whose swing speed is 62mph against 84mph for an average male golfer; 96mph for a typical LPGA professional and 108mph for an average PGA Tour player. At his peak big-hitting Tiger Woods was regularly recorded at 130mph with Rory McIlroy lagging behind on a high reading of 123.43. Even two-time Masters champion Bubba Watson only managed 128.17 but all are considered slowcoaches against the 148-152mph recorded by any winner of the World long drive competition.

## THE DANGERS OF LISTENING TO HEAVY METAL

Most golfers have to worry about lightning or being hit by a stray ball. But with the advent of the larger titanium drivers we now have something else to worry about – going deaf! A report in the *British Medical Journal* in 2009 discussed the possibility of the latest metal drivers causing a noise of sonic boom proportions, which according to one Edinburgh specialist can cause hearing problems if the golfer is subjected to it on a regular basis: 'Our results show that thin-faced titanium drivers may produce sufficient sound to induce temporary or even permanent cochlear damage in susceptible individuals,' said Dr Malcolm Buchanan.

## BOLT FROM THE BLUE!

The **British Ladies Golf Union** proposed in 1933 that its members should be able to take shelter should a thunderstorm break overhead during any medal competition; going against the wishes of the R&A, who saw dodging lightning as a breach of the rules entailing instant disqualification. They 'strongly advised' the LGU Executive Committee to abandon such a 'foolhardy' idea.

## PRESIDENT TEACHES PM HOW TO SPIN

Alastair Campbell, Chief Press Secretary to **British Prime Minister Tony Blair**, tried his hand at golf at St Andrews during the Commonwealth Heads of Government conference in May, 1997. One witness who saw him play described Mr Campbell's swing as 'like a caveman trying to kill his lunch!' During a visit to the United Kingdom for the same conference, U.S. President Bill Clinton gave Campbell's boss Tony Blair his first golf lesson. Clinton had spent the night at Chequers and after breakfast he could not resist a few holes of golf on the nearby Ellesborough Golf course. Blair joined the president for four holes and Clinton was full of praise for his golfing skills. Showing him the basics of stance, grip and swing, he expressed his admiration at the easy way Blair managed to impart backspin on the ball: 'Either he is an unbelievable athlete,' he said. 'Or I have a career as a golf instructor! One of the two things must be true…'

## TOP HEAVY!

A golfing **brassiere** went on sale in Japan in 2009. Proving popular with the sports-mad Japanese, the item of clothing concealed a 1.5m-long putting mat and included a built-in speaker which called out 'Nice shot' after every holed putt! The bra also features pockets for extra golf balls and tees, and a detachable flag pin that serves as a score pencil. For serious golfers, it also comes with a skirt with the words 'Be Quiet!' printed on the rear.

## BATTLING BLONDE IN PIGTAILS GETS BANNED

Top female professional Jane **Blalock** was suspended for virtually half of the 1972 season by the Executive Committee of the Ladies Professional Golf Association (LPGA). Found guilty of: 'actions inconsistent with the code of ethics of the organisation'. It followed her disqualification from the Bluegrass Invitational in Louisville, Kentucky, in May. Accused of improving her lie on the putting green, twenty-nine of her fellow players signed a petition calling for the LPGA to suspend her, which it did a few weeks later.

Leading the Official Money List at the time, Miss Blalock hit back by winning won a temporary court order that allowed her to compete in the LPGA Championship at the Pleasant Valley Country Club in Massachusetts. Never the most popular of players, she was openly snubbed by a number of fellow competitors but still finished second. Attracting worldwide interest, the story went into overdrive when she countered with a $5-million antitrust lawsuit against the LPGA in July. Described as a 'battling blonde in pigtails,' officials admitted placing binocular-wielding spotters behind trees and on television towers to gather evidence against the twenty-six-year old. Miss Blalock later conceded that she may have accidentally moved her ball 'through carelessness or excitement,' but suggested the draconian suspension was aimed at 'exterminating' her as the circuit's top money winner! In a game that survives on integrity, the ban and subsequent court case caused much debate in golfing circles. Blalock won her case in 1975 and was awarded $13,500 in damages and $90,000 in legal fees. After the verdict, the LPGA hired their first commissioner to deal with controversies involving players rather than a committee of fellow players. Blalock retired in 1986 with twenty-seven victories in her eighteen years on the LPGA Tour. Effectively playing under a cloud for the remainder of her professional career, she is still waiting to be inducted into the World Golf Hall of Fame.

## PAPER TIGERS

In the final practice round of the **Open** Championship at Muirfield in July 1987, a group of young English pros decided to have some fun at the expense of the R&A. Robert Lee, Mark Roe and Neil Hansen began by teeing-off the first with exploding golf balls – much to the annoyance of legends Gary Player, Arnold Palmer and Jack Nicklaus in the group behind. During the same round, the terrible trio decided to wear paper bags on their heads with the eyes cut out. Hitting shots with the new headgear proved tricky and resulted in a few mistimed strikes. As they got towards the end of the round, they swapped headwear with some scoreboard operators. Now wearing oversized tartan Tam O' Shanters, the entire group walked down the last to much

applause. Unfortunately, the R&A did not see the funny side and strongly reprimanded each one.

## HEAVENS ABOVE!

Dr Wilson, the **Bishop of Chelmsford** declared golf a self-serving, individualistic non-sport. 'A man who plays nothing else but golf cannot call himself a sportsman,' he said in a speech in London in 1935. 'I do not think we learn much from golf except the things one ought not to learn. As a golfer a man simply plays for himself. In other games, like football and cricket, he must blot himself out as an individual.'

## BABE BOOMS IT!

Mildred **'Babe'** Didrikson went on a much-publicised tour of the United States in 1935. Joined by reigning Masters Champion, Gene Sarazen, the former Olympic athlete delighted the galleries with powerful drives and a willingness to sign autographs. Happy to play the clown to Sarazen's straight man, when someone asked, 'How do you get such tremendous distance on your drives?' she replied in typically blunt style, 'I just loosen my girdle and let the ball have it!'

## EXTRA HOLES AT SUNNINGDALE

At the height of the **Battle of Britain** in September, 1940, James Sheridan, caddie master at Sunningdale Golf Club in Surrey, was mowing the 18th green on the Old Course. He had covered just over half of it when he heard two huge explosions from over the road on the Ladies Course. Realising the bombs were landing in a line, he threw himself into a greenside bunker. In the next three minutes, over fifty bombs rained down on the golf course and surrounding area. It turned out that a German aircraft had been attacked by a Spitfire and the crew had immediately ditched their bombs for a speedy escape. With the clubhouse barely touched, the indomitable Sheridan climbed out of his greenside bunker, dusted himself off and finished mowing the green.

## HELP! HELLO, GOODBYE

John Lennon, Paul McCartney, Ringo Star and George Harrison of the **Beatles** were thrown out of a Carlisle Golf Club dance in 1963 after they entered the clubhouse wearing leather jackets.

## STAND TO ATTENTION YOU CADS!

General **Billport** and Colonel **Brandell** had the reputation of being the meanest golfers in London in the 1940s. They would arrive at Richmond golf course near London around 10.30 a.m. each morning. At that time there were about forty caddies all waiting for jobs but the instant the two Army officers appeared there was a stampede away from the

caddie shed! Only the newest or youngest of bagmen could be induced to carry for these two men. Their tight-fisted behaviour was legendary. They would repaint their own golf balls rather than pay a caddie to do so. During the round if they chipped a piece out of the gutta ball they would stop the game while they placed a lighted match against the affected part and when sufficiently heated, rolled the ball in the palms of the hands so it could be used again. They would take four-and-a-half hours to complete a round, then take another two hours to play seven holes after lunch. They would often take an hour to look for a lost ball. Worse still, they paid only sixpence a round and threepence lunch money for the caddie, when other members would pay a shilling for the round and sixpence for lunch. They would bring their own lunch but order the caddie to borrow a plate from the clubhouse. If displeased with a caddie, they would cut his wages in half before reporting the miscreant to the caddie master, 'Old' Eli, and have them banned from the course for a week!

## FRIES WITH THAT BURGER?

**Bruce Burger** almost became one when he was dragged into a pond on the sixth hole at Lake Venice Golf Course in Florida. In June 2007 an eleven-foot long alligator decided he was lunch. Despite warning signs, Burger reached down to fish out his ball when the large reptile latched onto his right forearm and pulled him in. Using his left arm

to free himself he managed to call for help and was taken to a nearby Medical Centre where doctors managed to save his arm. The attack was the second in eighteen years at the Florida course. The other occurred when a player went into the same pond to retrieve a golf ball. 'Unfortunately, that's part of the Florida lifestyle,' a spokesman said. 'The bottom line is there's wildlife in them there ponds.'

## GONE FOR A BURTON!

The first **British Open** after the Second World War was scheduled for the Old Course at St Andrews in 1946. Defending champion Dick **Burton** sent in his entry accompanied by a note saying: 'I shall bring the Cup with me…' It seemed the famous old claret jug had been in his possession for six years since 1939. Then, having waited so long to defend his title, he sliced out-of-bounds at the first and was never in contention. In contrast, American Sam Snead had never been to St Andrews before but compiled four steady rounds to beat Bobby Locke and Johnny Bulla to win by four shots with a 290 total. Unlike Burton, he did not endear himself to the St Andrews crowd before or after the championship. His first comment on the ancient course was, 'it looks like an old abandoned kinda place…' He then had to be tracked down at his hotel for the trophy presentation! No real surprise then that he didn't turn up the following year to defend his title.

## CHATEAUBRIANDED

British Prime Minister David Lloyd George and his French counterpart, Aristide **Briand** met in Cannes in late April, 1921. A hastily arranged conference with representatives of former wartime enemy Germany, they were there to press the German government into paying already agreed war reparations under the Treaty of Versailles. Known for his love of golf, a round was organised at nearby Cannes Golf Club in which Lloyd George offered non-golfer Briand some tips on how to swing the club. Like every rookie golfer, he swung and missed. He became the butt of every French cartoonist; and the home press was highly critical of Briand taking instruction from Lloyd George, as it gave a 'subservient' impression to the

French electorate! Recalled to Paris in disgrace by French President Millerand, his disaster was compounded after Pathé News showed his golfing efforts in every cinema in Europe for weeks to come. Not surprisingly, he never picked up a golf club again.

## GOLF STOLE MY BRAIN!

George **Burns** found himself thinking the unthinkable prior to the final round of the 1979 Tournament Players Championship in Florida. Arriving on the first tee, the experienced PGA Tour Professional was only three shots behind the leader Lanny Wadkins. Setting up to the ball he suddenly forgot how to play! It was absurd, but no matter how much he tried, he could not get comfortable enough to make a swing. With his playing partners waiting patiently on the tee, the situation became desperate. Eventually he managed to move the ball forward and somehow scrambled around in 83. Describing it as 'the worst day of my life' Burns even considered walking off halfway through the round. The following week he scored 67 in the opening round at the Heritage Classic and the crisis was over.

## NEEDING A LEG UP

In a bizarre accident in the third round of the 1991 British Open at Royal Birkdale, English professional Richard **Boxall** was three shots off the lead when he collapsed in great pain. Teeing off at the ninth he suddenly screamed in agony. Playing partner Colin Montgomerie called for an ambulance and it was later diagnosed that he had broken his leg. He had woken up with an aching leg but thought it was just a twinge: 'I was out for ten months,' the Sky Television pundit recalled, 'I went from the comfort zone of having a few quid behind me to needing the money.'

## FAIRWAY, WHAT FAIRWAY?

Angus Hambro was drawn against an ex-naval officer from Scotland in the British Amateur **Championship** at Royal North Devon Golf Club in 1931. To the surprise of everyone, the officer arrived on the first tee armed with a four-foot-long ship's telescope. Then before each shot he pulled it out of his golf bag and pointed it down the fairway to get a better view. Hambro, one of the best amateur golfers in Britain, was so upset that he nearly lost the match and his temper.

## HALF CUT!

Percy **Chubb** was a hugely wealthy American businessman who liked nothing more than playing high-stake golf matches. In December 1931, he was playing another millionaire businessman for $100 a hole and $500 on the match. In an attempt to get out of a bunker his opponent had the misfortune to cut his ball in half with his niblick. A dispute ensued as to what should be done. Chubb insisted that he should play with the bigger half, as Rule 24 dealing with a replacement ball did not apply to any shot in a bunker. Unable to settle the dispute amicably they retired to the clubhouse, where they searched for the Club Captain to give a ruling. Failing to locate him, Chubb had the idea of sending a reply-paid cable to the Secretary of the Royal and Ancient Golf Club in St Andrews for a definitive opinion. Imbibing cocktails while they awaited the answer, the point at issue soon became immaterial as both became so drunk they were unable to continue!

## SOFT TOUCH ARNIE

In the 1962 **Colonial Tournament** Arnold Palmer was reading a putt at a crucial moment when a little boy in the crowd made some noise, forcing him to step away. As he readdressed his putt the boy started up again. The horrified mother put her hand over the son's mouth to shut him up after Arnie drew back once more. Walking over to the mother and son he patted the boy gently on the head and said, 'Hey, don't choke him; it's not that important!'

## COPY CATS IN THE BAG

Three **crooks** who engineered one of the biggest golf counterfeiting scams ever known were sentenced to a total of three years in English prison. The ruling came after Havering Council near London extradited two suspects from Thailand to face trial. Found guilty on 12 July 2013, the gang sold masses of fake clubs, accessories and other equipment to unsuspecting British golfers via virtual shops on the eBay auction website. Raking in sales of over $3 million, Raymond Crook, Brian Ferrigno and Paul Biggerstaff were sentenced respectively to nine, ten and eighteen months' imprisonment. The massive investigation, codenamed 'Augusta', began after a complaint in 2005 from a member of the public who was unhappy with the quality of their clubs.

## BILLY NO MATES

William 'Billy' **Casper**, the 1970 Masters Champion, invoked his right as a past champion to play at Augusta National. Telling the press he intended to play just one round on 7 April 2005, the seventy-three-year old recorded the worst ever score in Masters History with a 106 (34 over par) – a score that included a 14 on the par 3 16th! Not surprisingly Casper did not hand in his card and was subsequently disqualified, so the round did not stand in the official tournament statistics. 'I just had to get it out of my system,' he said afterward. Sensibly, the Masters committee reviewed its policy of automatically allowing past champions to take part.

## GOLF GETS CARBONARA'D

A **cablegram** from the British Embassy in Rome in January 1934 described how the Italian Golf Federation had gone 'ultra-nationalist'. This meant that all British citizens were banned from golf courses throughout Italy with all-non Italians forced to pay a special tax to obtain an identity card before being permitted to play. Worse still, British phrases like 'slice', 'hook', 'par' and 'bunker' were also banned. 'If Signor Mussolini insists that visiting golfers shall change their plus fours and Fair Island pullovers for riding breeches and a black shirt,' said the editor of *Golf Illustrated* magazine, 'then he is sadly mistaken.'

## GAMBLING GOLFER

Archie **Compston**, well-known professional golfer and coach to HRH Edward, Prince of Wales, was taken to court in May over tax irregularities relating to his earnings in 1928. Challenged over the amount of £1,000 won in side bets, it was stated that Compston had habitually engaged in private games for the past decade or more. Playing mainly against well-heeled amateurs, these money matches took place as

often as three or four times a week for as much as £50 to £100 per game. As Compston rarely lost, the accusation was the money earned should be taxed as income. In his defence, it was argued that if he were not a professional, but a top amateur, the position would be different. Presiding over the case, Mr Justice Lawrence agreed and declared in the Revenue Court of the King's Bench Division in London that any money wagered and won by Mr Compston should not be taxable — no matter how high the figure may be. After all, if an ordinary golfer had a bet, either with a friend or a bookmaker, his winnings were not taxable, and neither could he make deductions for income-tax purposes respecting his losses.

## GOOSE-STEPPING GOLF

When does cutting-edge art dip into the murky world of bad taste? Some would say when it combines the two words 'golf' and 'Adolf Hitler' in the same sentence. Putting their own twist on the family-friendly theme of mini-golf, controversial Brit artists Jake and Dinos **Chapman** put together an exhibition called 'Adventureland Golf' at the

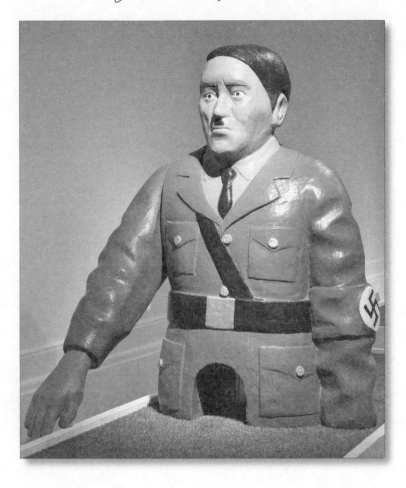

Grundy Art Gallery in Blackpool in August 2012. Featuring art as crazy golf course obstacles, the one that attracted most attention was their lifelike figure of Hitler which raised its arm in a Nazi salute every time the ball passed between its legs! Condemned by Michael Samuels of the Board of Deputies of British Jews as 'tasteless' and with 'no artistic value whatsoever' the gallery described it as a 'powerful image of the Nazi regime within the context of holiday fun'. Defending the artists' 'right to offend' they added: 'We do not have the right, as citizens, to be free from every image that upsets, shocks, or even disgusts us. To call this crazy golf representation of Adolf Hitler tasteless is a bit like calling the Colossus of Rhodes colossal!' Proving that nothing sells better than controversy, the only 'colossal' thing about this golfing art, according to most people, was the price tag…

## GUN SHY

The legendary Walter Hagen was playing at **Detroit Golf Club** with Edsel Bryant Ford, President of the Ford Motor Company, in May 1928 (he was the only son of its founder, Henry Ford). At one point, Edsel called to his caddie to bring over his bag. Unzipping a pocket he fumbled around inside looking for a golf

SPORT KINGS GUM

WALTER HAGEN

ball when without warning a .38 automatic pistol dropped on the ground! 'I drew back in pretended alarm,' Hagen recalled years later. 'Edsel,' I said, 'If you want this hole so badly, I'll concede!' Ford then explained the gun was a result of recent kidnapping threats.

## SPEED FREAKS

Sponsored by a **Detroit radio** station in 2008, a group of forty local golfers set a record for the fastest ever round at 7 minutes, 56 seconds. Strategically located along the tee boxes, fairways and greens, they played tag-team style with players running to the ball as soon as it came to rest. When a putt was holed out, another was immediately put into play on the next tee.

## A LAW UNTO HIMSELF

After a series of clubhouse thefts in St Andrews in July 1931, local youth Bob Alva Pittar was arrested and brought before Hamilton Magistrates Court on 22 August. **Detective-Sergeant** Thompson said that visiting golfers had complained about missing money that they had left in their clothes in the changing rooms. A sting operation was set for the visit of a team from Hamilton Golf Club and the accused was seen extracting a marked 10 shilling note from a coat owned by Mr W. J. King. The eighteen-year-old was arrested before admitting to a string of other thefts. The magistrate, Mr Wyvern Wilson, said there were some unpleasant features about the case. The accused had mixed with his father's friends in order to secure admission to the clubhouse, and he had deliberately and with premeditation stolen the money. Mr Pittar was given probation for two years on the strict condition that he made full restitution of all the monies stolen.

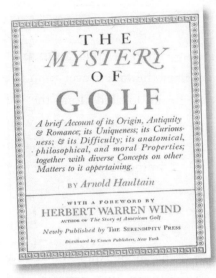

THE
MYSTERY
O F
GOLF

*A brief Account of its Origin, Antiquity
& Romance; its Uniqueness; its Curious-
ness; & its Difficulty; its anatomical,
philosophical, and moral Properties;
together with diverse Concepts on other
Matters to it appertaining.*

BY *Arnold Haultain*

WITH A FOREWORD BY
HERBERT WARREN WIND
AUTHOR OF *The Story of American Golf*

*Newly Published by* THE SERENDIPITY PRESS
*Distributed by Crown Publishers, New York*

## JUST DO IT!

The *American Golfer* magazine published a list of 'Do's and Don'ts in Golf' by Arnold Haultain, author of *The Mystery of Golf*, in its January 1911 edition:

*1. Don't hurry—either before the game—or during the game—or after the game; otherwise you will contract the habit.*

*2. Don't hurry your stroke: time is of the essence of the impact.*

*3. Don't mind who your opponent may be; and*

*4. Don't watch your opponent; you are playing your game; let him play his.*

*5. Don't worry about your caddie. He may be an irritating little wretch; but for eighteen holes he is your caddie; accordingly*

*6. Don't lose your temper—about anything, anything whatsoever.*

*If you lose your temper, you lose everything—self-control, self-respect, judgment, equanimity, decency of language—and, of course, the hole, and probably the game.*

7. *Don't watch the pair behind—even if they drive into you. You can complain afterwards.*

8. *Don't experiment—unless you are in a desperate difficulty—or are dormy.*

9. *Don't talk. If your opponent talks,*

10. *Don't listen to your opponent. Edge away from him. If your caddie talks,*

11. *Don't listen to your caddie; shut him up.*

12. *Don't fuss. Fussiness is inimical to seriousness.*

13. *Don't fidget. Fidgetiness is inimical to steadiness.*

14. *Don't argue. The rules are the rules. A moot point can be reserved.*

15. *Don't debate—even with yourself; there is the hole; there are your clubs.*

16. *Don't hesitate. Hesitation evinces weakness, and your opponent will notice it.*

17. *Don't be too polite; and*

18. *Don't be too sympathetic; golf is a combat.*

19. *Don't be cast down; it spoils one's game. On the other hand,*

20. *Don't be elated; that, too, spoils one's game. Whether you are 'up' or whether you are 'down,'*

21. *Don't vary your game.*

22. *Don't put on airs. Lastly, and above all,*

23. *Don't take your eye off your ball—never.*

## BRING BACK PLUS FOURS I SAY!

**Denim jeans** proved a real point of controversy with the fashion police at Detroit Golf Club in Michigan. In November 2014 they announced the longstanding ban on denim clothing would no longer be enforced. Founded in 1899, Detroit Golf Club Board of Directors notified club members in an email that denim, defined as a 'coarse, twilled sturdy cotton cloth used for jeans', could henceforth be worn on club grounds as long as it was not 'ripped or torn (and) must be tasteful and appropriate for a club environment'. But in a final nod to decades of banned denim clothing it was announced that DGC members and guests may not enter the clubhouse through the front entrance in jeans declaring that 'The Professional Shop or side entries may be used.'

## AN ORIGINAL ABORIGINAL GOLF COURSE

The world's first so-called '**extreme**' golf course opened on 11 July 1935, near Darwin, Australia. Hacked out of a mangrove swamp with the help of Aboriginal prisoners from the nearby Fannie Bay Prison, fairways ran down avenues of thick jungle. Tees were cut into the bamboo thickets ten feet tall with many of the greens surrounded by twenty-foot-high pandanus palms. As a former swamp, thousands of large land crabs crawled out at night and burrowed holes into the fairway. The clearing of the jungle also exposed many sweet roots, which attracted wallabies and bandicoots that dug deep holes from which it was difficult to hack out a golf ball. In addition, hawks and kites were always on the look-out for golf balls and carried them away into the

GOLF IN OTHER LANDS
AUSTRALIA
© THE GERLACH BARKLOW CO. JOLIET, ILL

jungle. Add to the mix deadly snakes, spiders and scorpions and making a par became less of a challenge than actually surviving the round. No wonder then that Fannie Bay Links did not survive the Second World War.

## TRAFFIC STOPPER

Four days after his inauguration on 24 January 1953, President Dwight D. **Eisenhower** was spotted on the back lawn of the White House practising his short irons in the direction of the Washington Monument. Despite his request for a simple inaugural parade, his wishes were ignored. Described in the *New York Times* as 'the biggest, flashiest, most expensive and impressive Inauguration party of them all', it featured an Alaskan dog team, three elephants and a float depicting 'Ike' playing golf. In a letter to Augusta National Head Pro Ed Dudley dated 20 February, 'Ike' describes stopping traffic while practising his golf. '(My) Practice is beginning to cause some congestion on the street about 275 yards away from where the spectators use field glasses and telescope lenses. I don't mind being watched but I do hate to block traffic. If the public doesn't lose interest in my divot digging pretty soon I shall have to give it up.'

## JFK G.C.

**Evangelist** Billy Graham was known to have played with Senator John F. Kennedy at Seminole in January 1961 just days before JFK's Presidential inauguration. 'For me,' JFK said, 'a golf course is an island of peace in a world often full of confusion and turmoil.'

## NOT SO HONOURABLE

In 1776 The Honourable Company of **Edinburgh** Golfers banned the amount one golfer could win off another in a day's play. It seemed that far too many duels were being fought between members to settle their disputes! Unfortunately, this ruling did not allow for the ingenuity of some members who soon found a way around it. With the limit set on how much you could win in 'one-day's play', matches were played over three holes at night with the caddies holding a lantern to show the way!

## PUSHED TO THE LIMIT

Chicago stockbroker James Smith-**Ferebee** completed a sponsored four-day transcontinental golfing jaunt on 4 October 1937. Taking in Los Angeles, Phoenix, Kansas City, St Louis, Milwaukee, Chicago, Philadelphia and New York, he covered 3,000 miles by plane and tramped over 155 miles on foot. Playing 600 holes, he wore out two dozen pair of gloves but remarkably did not lose a ball. Accompanied by his eighteen-year-old caddie Art Cashetta, his personal physician, Dr Charles B. Alexander (who fed him orange juice and water), and his financial backer Reuben Trane (who had 3,000 autographed golf balls handed out en route advertising his air-conditioning business), he finished at 10.30 p.m. at Salisbury Country Club on Long Island on a green lit by magnesium

flares. Quite the showman, J.M. Ferebee played his 601st hole on the stroke of midnight at New York's World's Fair Grounds. Taking the applause of the crowd he then headed to a swanky Manhattan hotel where he hung a sign on his bedroom door: 'Don't open until Christmas.' The following day, the *New York Times* announced that he had taken 2,860 strokes with his lowest score 77 and highest 99.

## SCORECARD SCANDAL

Showman and world-class self-publicist Willie **Fumpson** caused a sensation when he reputedly scored a single round of 51 (23-under par) on the Ngaruawahia golf course in New Zealand in his first ever round of golf! With the feat reported globally there was even talk of a lucrative American tour being offered where he would go head-to-head with

Walter Hagen and Bobby Jones. With reporters chasing him for his 'secret' Fumpson finally came clean about his incredible round. 'I noticed that everyone was trying to put the ball down every single hole,' he said. 'I thought what a waste of energy! So after a little deep thinking, I decided to go straight from the first green to the eighteenth green, which is 20 yards away. I took 51 strokes to reach it, but that was enough to break the course record!'

## CUBAN HEELS

**Fidel Castro** played golf at Colinas de Villareal Golf Club with the legendary Ernesto 'Che' Guevara shortly after the Cuban missile crisis in October 1962 (see photo, page 52). It was said that Castro intended to send a defiant message to United States President John F. Kennedy by showing it was life as normal in post-revolutionary Cuba. While Castro came from a wealthy family whose members did play golf, he was not thought to have played himself. Guevara in contrast had regular contact with the sport as a caddy in his Argentine hometown before he became a guerrilla icon. Apparently he beat Castro and a journalist who reported this was fired the next day. El Presidente then ordered that Havana Golf Club be turned into a military school and another private club into an art school. Talk about a bad loser…

## DEAD LIE

A **free funeral** was the prize on offer for any professional who made a hole-in-one on the eighth hole at the 1985 New South Wales Open in Australia.

## GATECRASHING THE OPEN

Maurice **Flitcroft**, a forty-six-year-old crane driver from Barrow-in-Furness, entered the British Open at Royal Birkdale in July 1976. The only problem was that he had only taken up the game sixteen months earlier! Playing with a cheap half-set of golf clubs he had bought from a newspaper he was determined to find 'fame and fortune' in the Open at Birkdale. Not having a handicap he ticked the box for 'professional' and headed for the qualifying rounds at Formby. Not surprisingly he took 121 strokes and was immediately disqualified. A huge embarrassment to the R&A, the £30 entry fee was refunded to his two furious

playing partners. Forced to tighten up entry procedures, the R&A thwarted Flitcroft when he entered again in 1983 under the nom-de-plume of Gerard Hoppy.

## SHORT FUSE!

American professional **Forrest Fezler** was admonished by the USGA after wearing shorts during the practice rounds of the 1984 U.S. Open at Oakmont, PA. Annoyed at having to change into pants he stripped back into navy-blue shorts for the final hole! He remains the only pro to have worn shorts in a major championship.

## CASH ACCUMULATOR

Jim **Furyk** holed the most expensive putt ever on the final green to win the 2010 Tour Championship at East Lake in Atlanta, Georgia. Getting down in two from a greenside bunker for par, his three-footer gave him a par round of 70 and a one-stroke victory over Luke Donald, who also shot a 70. Exactly a month after he was disqualified from the Barclays tournament after oversleeping and missing his pro-am start time, Furyk pocketed $1.35 million for winning the tournament and a $10 million bonus – a combined total of $11,350,000 in prize money – for finishing top of the FedEx Cup end-of-season rankings.

## KING OF PUTTERS

The longest known putt in golf history is attributed to sixty-six-year old amateur **Fergus Muir.** Playing the downwind 125-yard par 3 fifth hole at St Andrew's Eden Course on 6

November 2001, he holed out for an ace using an antique hickory putter. Classed as a putt by *The Guinness Book of Records*, it was officially measured at 375 feet.

## COME BACK TOMORROW, FOLKS

Jim **Furyk** and Scott Hoch were on the second playoff hole in the 2003 Doral Tournament in Florida when Hoch informed PGA Tour officials that he couldn't properly read his birdie putt. With the green in semi-darkness and light fading fast, his request to halt the playoff was granted at 6:33 p.m. Greeted by a chorus of boos from the large crowd who had waited all day to see a conclusion to the tournament, the two pros returned to the course the following Monday morning. Then, in front of a sparse crowd, Hoch won on the third extra hole to pick up a $500,000 cheque.

## FOREPLAY

An errant shot during a friendly game descended into an eight-year legal battle over whether or not shouting **'Fore!'** offered any protection in law. Appearing before the Court of Appeals in New York two doctors described how they were playing at Dix Hills Park Golf Course, New York, in October 2002. Playing from the rough, Dr Anoop Kapoor accidentally struck Dr Azad Anand in the head leaving him permanently blinded in one eye. He accused Dr Kapoor of not shouting the traditional warning of 'Fore!' and the case went to court. The judge found against Dr Anand saying that golf was inherently dangerous and dismissed any claims

for damages. From there it went to the Appellate Division, who also decided that Dr Kapoor had no legal obligation to yell 'Fore!' on a crowded golf course. (Kapoor claimed that he did shout a warning after he struck his shot but this was denied by Anand and another golfing partner.) The case is still ongoing.

## SEA TO SHINING SEA HOLE

American **Floyd Satterlee Rood** played a single hole from the Pacific West Coast of America to the Atlantic Coast 3,397.7 miles away. Playing from 14 September to 3 October 1962, he took 114,737 strokes and lost 3,511 balls!

## ALL ABOARD!

Ross Sobel invented a new form of golf in 1965 for cruise ships and leisure resorts called the **'Floating Golf Game'**. It involved hitting a feather light ball onto floating greens set in a small round pool. Based on a similar game invented in the 1930s it proved popular for a short time after the first one was laid out on the deck of the SS *Ariadne*, a passenger liner that toured the Bahamas and the Caribbean.

## THOSE MAGNIFICENT MEN IN THEIR FLYING MACHINES

An unusual golf society sprung up in England in 1919 – the **Flyers Golfing Club**. Born out of RAF combat missions in the First World War the only rule was players must travel by aeroplane covering a minimum of 100 miles in the air before playing. The first competition was held at Royal West

Norfolk Golf Course in Brancaster and heralded by two De Havilland Moths landing noisily on the eighteenth fairway!

## HARRASSING HAGEN

Noted journalist **Grantland Rice** wrote a critical article about Walter Hagen for *Collier's* Magazine in 1930 entitled: 'Golf's Bad Boy'. Known for his close friendship with Hagen's biggest rival Bobby Jones, Rice dragged up hoary old stories of Hagen in an obvious attempt to reinforce his already dubious reputation for gamesmanship and unprofessional behaviour. Recalling Hagen's decision to change his shoes in his motor car rather than the locker room at Deal in 1920, his habit of arriving late for important matches like his World Championship Challenge match against Abe Mitchell in England in 1926, Rice described him as the 'stormy petrel of golf, one of the most widely praised and one of the most keenly criticised competitors in

any game…' For some golf fans he was: 'one of the greatest fellows.' For others he had been 'a goat-getter and a bum!'

## GO FOR IT GLORIA

**Gloria Minoprio** caused a sensation at the English Women's Golf Championship in October 1933. In the days when a shapely ankle caused apoplexy among male golfers, she turned up to play in a beret, turtleneck sweater and matching black trousers instead of a skirt! Arriving in a yellow Rolls-Royce, she added to the clubhouse gossip by turning up to play using just one club – a long-shafted straight faced iron, a 'cleek' – with her caddie carrying a spare in case it broke! Later the same year, she added to her rebellious reputation by wearing waterproof trousers in a Women's event at Stoke Poges in Buckinghamshire. Not that she did not have support from her fellow female golfers; 'I just wish that trousers had been in vogue in my day,' said 1929 British Ladies champion, Joyce Wethered. 'Skirts were such a problem… They would fall just above the ankle, and you had to be very careful that they were tight enough not to flap, yet loose enough to let you take up your stance.' The Ladies Golf Union of Great Britain reacted to the 'Minoprio' controversy by issuing a statement that: 'deplored any departure from the traditional costume of ladies'.

## SWINGTIME

Top American star **Gene Sarazen** set out to prove that noise no more distracts a golfer than crowd noise puts off a batter at baseball. Playing an exhibition match at the Shorehaven

Golf Club in Connecticut in 1940 with fellow pro Jimmy Demaret, boxer Gene Tunney and baseball legend Babe Ruth, Sarazen served up some fairly novel distractions. Employing Fred Waring and his swing band, he ordered them to play it 'loud and clear' as the four players teed off at every hole! Accompanied by a bemused crowd of 5,000 spectators, each one was invited to cheer the good shots and boo the bad ones. In the end Demaret and Ruth beat Sarazen and Tunney, 2 & 1. Demaret shot a par 72, Sarazen 73, Ruth and Tunney 82 each. The gallery voted it more fun than a circus.

## A REAL GOLF BANDIT

The St Andrews Golf Club in Scotland installed a new **gambling** machine in 1959 which paid out winners in brand new golf balls. Its introduction was not trouble-free as the Auchterlonie Golf Shop protested about a loss of sales. The machine was finally removed from the clubhouse a few months later after some less-than-honest members found out how to cheat the machine and acquire free golf balls!

## HEADACHE FOR HITLER

Arnold Bentley from Hesketh in Lancashire and Yorkshireman Tommy Thirsk represented England at the **Grosser Golfpreis der Nationen** (Great Golf Prize of Nations). Held ten days after the Berlin Olympic Games ended, on 16 August 1936, the tournament was sponsored by the Nazi Government who saw it as a propaganda opportunity. Hosted by the Baden-Baden Golf Club in the

Black Forest area of Germany, seven countries participated, each represented by a pair of golfers. The format was 72 holes of stroke play over two days with the aggregate score of both players counting. The home country was represented by nineteen-year-old Leonard von Beckerath and C.A. Helmers. After thirty-six holes, the Germans led by three strokes, five shots clear of England and ten in front of France. A possible victory for the German team saw Adolf Hitler heading for Baden-Baden to present the trophy. But with the Reich Chancellor assured that a glorious home victory was all but certain, Thirsk and Bentley dominated the final two rounds, helped in no small part by consecutive rounds of 65 by Thirsk. In the end they beat the Germans by twelve strokes and the French by four - forcing an embarrassed Foreign Minister Von Ribentropp to make a mad dash to intercept Hitler's car to turn him back. Thirsk

and Bentley were then presented with the trophy by Karl Henkell, president of the German Golf Federation, (DGV).

## TREE TROUBLE

A British Golf Club had a veritable forest of trees stolen in May 2013. **Green keepers** at Crane Valley Golf Club in Dorset turned up to work at 5.45am to find that ninety-one newly planted leylandii trees had been dug up by their roots and taken overnight. The trees were all between five and seven feet tall and according to police had a combined value of less than £900.

## MOTHER'S PRIDE

**Gamesmanship** is fairly commonplace in golf but few ruses have reached the depths of the head-to-head battle between William Serrick and Raymond McAuliffe at Salisbury Golf Club, New York, in 1925. As they stood on the first tee waiting to begin their afternoon round, a Western Union courier dashed up with a message for Serrick. Visibly upset, he put the cablegram in his pocket before losing 6 & 5 to his cigar-chomping opponent. Walking off the green he was stunned to see his mother in the gallery. Unable to control his emotions he hugged her and showed her the telegram. Believed to be from his opponent or one of his supporters, it read: 'MOTHER DANGEROUSLY ILL. PLEASE COME AT ONCE.'

## GREEN INITIATIVE

American Ryder Cup golfer Ken **Green** made history in April 2010 when he became the first professional in history to compete in an official PGA Tour Seniors event with a prosthetic leg. Ten months earlier he suffered a major car accident when a tyre on his camper van blew on a Mississippi highway, the subsequent crash killing both his girlfriend and his brother. His lower right leg had to be amputated. As if that was not enough, Green discovered that his son Hunter had died of a drugs overdose while he was undergoing therapy. Partnering Mike Reid in the pairs tournament he played well enough to finish twenty-sixth. Asked what it was like, fifty-year-old Green said: 'Imagine Eric Clapton having to learn to play guitar left-handed and then performing "Layla" in front of 10,000 fans!'

## TAKING ALL DAY

**Glen Day** of Australia was penalised one shot for a 'pace of play violation' following the third round of the Honda Classic on 11 March 1995. Playing with Mark O'Meara, their round took over four hours to complete with O'Meara complaining of having to wait on almost every shot. Known as 'All Day' because of his lacklustre pace of play, his score was adjusted from his actual 71 to 72, and he finished twenty-fourth in the event.

## EXPENSIVE ROUND OF GOLF

A **German** golfer racked up a phone bill of more than £2,000 ($3,200) by using a golf app on his mobile while holidaying abroad in May 2013. The unfortunate tourist played three rounds of golf and downloaded the GPS mapping data each time. Incurring huge overseas roaming data charges every time the app connected to his phone network, he only found out when he returned home and was presented with a £2,025 bill.

## PICKPOCKETING PRESTON

An unusual bet took place at **Home Park** Golf Club next to Hampton Court in December 1925. Peter Kempley delayed driving off the sixth tee because 187 yards ahead of him in the rough was fellow member G. F. Preston. 'You would never hit him in a hundred years at this distance,' said his playing partner somewhat mischievously. Taking up a £5 wager at odds of 25 to 1, Kempley struck Mr Preston on the elbow. Running up the fairway to apologise, Preston said, 'I felt something hit me, but I cannot find your ball.' They searched for some time and finally found it in Mr Preston's pocket. How was that for accuracy?

## HACKED OFF!

Buddy **Hackett** described a round with fellow comedian Jimmy Durante in his 1968 book, *The Truth about Golf, and Other Lies*: 'Jimmy's first round was a total disaster,' he wrote. 'As he came to the eighteenth hole, his partner, who had long since lost count, estimated Jimmy's score was over 200. After holing out for 12, the Schnoz turned to his companion and asked, 'What should I give the caddie?' Without smiling, the friend answered, 'Your clubs!'

## TRUST ME I'M A GOLFER

In an 'attitudinal study' commissioned by **Hyatt Hotels & Resorts** in 1993 over half of the 401 businessmen surveyed admitted cheating at golf! Entitled 'Golf and the Business Executive' it investigated whether the way a person conducted their business affairs was similar to the way they played golf. It made fascinating reading with 55% admitting to cheating at least once. About the same percentage admitted calling in sick or leaving the office early to play golf. Other offences included improving a poor lie (41%); not counting a missed putt (19%); taking a mulligan and not counting the previous shot (13%); making one score and writing down another (8%); and dropping a new ball James Bond-style while pretending to look for a wayward one in the woods (6%). Perhaps most revealingly, just over one in ten agreed that golf was more important than sex!

## WHAT HOWARD HUGHES WANTS HOWARD HUGHES USUALLY GETS

The prestigious Tournament of Champions was moved from Nevada to California at the express request of billionaire **Howard Hughes**. Played at the (now defunct) Desert Inn Hotel & Country Club in Las Vegas since 1953, he purchased the property in 1968 and made the Penthouse Suite his home. Living in complete seclusion he became paranoid about the germs that would be released by the large crowds watching the action below if the tournament went ahead! Demanding the event be cancelled or moved elsewhere, it was hurriedly relocated to La Costa in California.

## GUILTY PLEASURES

**Howard B. Lee** was sued for divorce by his wife in 1925 citing his obsession with golf! A scratch golfer, he was the son of millionaire Detroit automobile dealer James L. Lee. Amazingly the judge, who was a golfer himself, agreed and ruled in her favour. Making legal history it was the first time an American court accepted a preoccupation with anything other than a mistress as reason for divorce and the application was granted on grounds of neglectful behaviour and mental cruelty.

## MEMBERS ONLY PLEASE

**Howard Hughes** story number two; the eccentric billionaire often upset the Wilshire Golf Club management in Los Angeles by showing up without a tee time and demanding a caddie without having reserved one. When they protested at his habit of bringing personal guests to the club, billionaire Hughes simply bought them memberships on the spot at the cost of many thousands of dollars. In 1926 Hughes hired reigning U.S. Amateur champion George Von Elm to help with his game. As a famed movie producer, he insisted his film crew record each practice session from every conceivable angle. He even attached a camera to a dirigible to film him golfing from above.

## A KNOCK TO THE ROYAL NOGGIN

**HRH** Prince William was admitted to the Royal Berkshire Hospital after being hit on the side of the forehead by a golf club! Taking lessons at Ludgrove School he was accidentally struck by a fellow pupil. The Prince did not lose consciousness but suffered a depressed fracture of the skull. Undergoing a four-hour operation at the Great Ormond Street Hospital, the mark is still visible and he has named it his 'Harry Potter scar'. On hearing the news Princess Diana raced to the hospital behind the ambulance. Controversy ensued the following morning after the British tabloids discovered that Prince Charles had left the hospital that night to attend the opera. Answering a question in 2009 about his scar, William said: 'We were on a putting green and the next thing you know there was a seven-iron and it came out of nowhere and it hit me in the head...'

## HEAD OVER HEELS OVER HEPBURN

Howard Hughes story number three: Oscar-winning actress Katharine **Hepburn** was enjoying a round with her instructor, Joe Novak at Bel-Air Country Club in October 1936. Looking up she spotted a low-flying, single-engine plane circling the Hollywood course. It soon became obvious the spiralling Sikorsky amphibian was piloted by playboy, movie mogul and her relentless suitor, Howard Hughes. Touching down on the eighth fairway he had come a-courting in the way only billionaires can! Refusing to acknowledge his daredevil antics, Hepburn barely broke her stride as she continued her round. Both keen players,

Hepburn often broke 80 while Hughes was a former 2 handicap golfer with delusions of turning pro. Climbing from his plane, thirty-year old Hughes approached the twenty-nine-year-old redhead on the tenth tee and simply asked, 'Mind a third?' Golf had drawn them together and became a constant subject of conversation during their numerous dinner dates together over the next three years. Theirs was a passionate, fiery romance. Hepburn once interrupted him mid-haircut and demanded they play golf. Hughes got out of the barber's chair with barely a thought, his head only half trimmed. 'I played for fun and exercise, Howard played always to improve his game,' she once recalled. 'He was slow… I finally used to be almost a hole ahead of him. I was busy admiring the sky, the flowers – the relaxation. He would be utterly disgusted with me: "You could be a really fine golfer if you would only practise." I used to think "and you could be fun if you weren't so slow."'

## SHALL WE CALL IT SQUARE?

Two members of the **Harewood Golf Club** in Christchurch, New Zealand set a new world record for a play-off – 80 holes – in 1935. Single-handicap golfer C. J. McFadden faced 14-handicap A. L. Kay. They set out at one o'clock on Saturday to play a match in the fifth round of the Blank Cup. All square after eighteen holes, they agreed to play another nine holes to settle the matter. Once again they finished all square. There was some daylight left so they agreed to settle the issue with another nine holes. For the third time they finished all square. On Sunday morning McFadden and Kay played another eighteen holes and again they finished all square. Another nine holes after lunch ended all square by which time they had attracted a small but interested gallery. After a short break they started another eighteen. Finally the match ended on the seventeenth green with McFadden the winner by 3 & 1.

## 'ALLO 'ALLO – WELCOME TO GOLF IN THE FATHERLAND

The National Socialist (Nazi) Party under Adolf **Hitler** believed that Western powers would look on their regime more favourably if they popularised golf in Germany. Boasting 42 private golf clubs in 1934 compared with 2,000 in England and Scotland, he ordered the exclusive clubs to slash their membership fee to two marks for adults and a nominal one mark for juniors. More public courses would be built and the cost of clubs and balls brought within the pocket of ordinary citizens. Appointing Party member Karl Henkel to oversee this rapid growth, he instigated a series of tournaments beginning with a national amateur championship.

## GOLF: MARKED FOR LIFE

**Hollywood star** Mark Wahlberg vowed never to star in a golf movie despite his obsession with the game. 'Golf is my passion,' he said in 2007. 'But here's no way I'd do a movie about it; all the ones that have been made, SUCK!'

## ACES HIGH!

A veritable feast of **hole-in-ones** were recorded in the United States in 1964. Even with odds against any amateur getting one at 6,000–1, a total of 11,774 aces were recorded. Examples were cited like an eighty-four-year-old retired businessman from California (No. 8 iron, 110-yard hole), a nine-year-old from North Carolina (No. 3 iron, 157-yard hole), and a Texas housewife who was eight months pregnant when she holed with a full 6-iron on a 125-yard hole. Other notable aces included Norman Manley from Inglewood, California, who scored three in a month - all on par fours of 330, 330 and 290 yards. Perhaps most unusual of all was Harry Poli, 56, who used a putter to ace a 150-yard hole in June at the Salem, Mass., Municipal Golf Course.

## NO HANDICAP FOR HOGAN

Ben **Hogan** was the Tiger Woods of golf in the late 1940s. Featured on the cover of *Time* magazine on 10 January 1949, he was only the third golfer to be honoured in this way. Then disaster struck. Exhausted by a long run of tournaments and exhibition matches he decided to drive from Arizona to his home at Fort Worth in Texas for a much needed rest before the Masters in April. It was a journey he would not complete.

On the night of 1 February, his Cadillac was involved in a car crash just outside a small, fog-shrouded Texas town named Van Horn. As they were crossing a two-lane bridge, Hogan's car collided head-on with a Greyhound bus that had swung into his lane to pass a truck. The impact drove the engine into the driver's seat and throwing himself over his wife, Ben took the full force of the collision with Valerie receiving only minor lacerations. It would take ninety minutes for an ambulance to reach the crash scene. Hogan was taken to a small clinic in Van Horn for X-rays, then by ambulance to the Hotel Dieu Hospital in El Paso, 150 miles away. He suffered internal bleeding and multiple fractures including a broken collarbone, a smashed rib, a double fracture of the pelvis and a broken ankle. Having survived, Hogan's health status was upgraded to 'good' on 17 February. Twenty-four hours later he suffered respiratory distress due to a large pulmonary embolus to the right lung. The same day he felt a sharp pain in his chest as three large blood clots formed in his legs and headed up to his lungs. He was not expected to live. The doctors were forced to operate in an effort to save him as his heart beat became erratic and his blood pressure dropped to dangerous levels. Told about a new procedure developed by a Dr Alton Ochsner he was flown by B52 bomber to Texas where Dr Ochsner performed a two-hour operation on the ailing golfer. Afterwards Valerie was told that her husband would never walk again or play golf! Recovery was slow and extremely painful as he lay in a hospital bed for almost two months. Then in one of the great miracles of sport: Hogan not only walked but returned to win the 1950 United States Open – just sixteen months after being severely injured.

## SPIDER LOOKING FOR A HOLM

Daniela **Holmqvist** felt a sharp pain in her ankle as she played in a pre-qualifier for the ISPS Handa Australian Open at the Royal Canberra Golf Club in Yarralumla, Australia, on 12 February 2013. When the Swedish twenty-four-year-old looked down she realised she'd been bitten by a black widow spider. Secreting poison through its fangs the arachnid is so venomous that its bite can kill an adult in under an hour! Doubled over in pain and with her leg swelling up, Holmqvist calmly reached into her pocket, pulled out a golf tee and used it to gash open her bite and squeezed the venom out! 'When I told the local caddies in my group what had happened, they immediately started looking for their phones to call the medics,' she said. Playing on through the pain she shot a 74 with medics following her around the course to make sure she didn't pass out. 'It still hurts,' Holmqvist said the following day. 'So I don't recommend getting bitten by a black widow.'

## A GEORGIA PEACH

Legendary author Ernest **Hemingway** attended the 1961 Masters tournament at Augusta National Golf Club barely three months before he committed suicide on 2 July in Ketchum, Idaho.

Not known as a golfer, the author thought the Georgia course was simply stunning and later said how the eighteenth hole reminded him of Mount Kilimanjaro in Africa, except there were golfers on it instead of leopards.

## HIGH FLYERS

Donald C. **Ildecott** of the Lancashire Aero Club took up William Eamsdon for a flight after they had enjoyed a morning round of golf together at Cheadle Hume G.C. near Manchester in northern England. Flying low over the course in an effort to 'buzz' their golfing pals below, the plane began to pitch and loop before falling like a stone. Pulled from the wreckage, both men sustained injuries but later made a full recovery.

## MY GRANNIE WOULD HAVE KNOCKED THAT ONE IN

Hale **Irwin** missed a tap-in putt on the fourteenth green during the third round of the 1983 British Open at Royal

Troon in Scotland. Barely five-inches from the hole, the right-handed golfer attempted to play it left-handed with the back of his putter. Taking a casual swipe the putter skipped off the ground behind the ball and literally jumped over it without moving it forward. Hardly able to believe what he had done, the shell-shocked American brushed the ball in with his next stroke. Costing the veteran American star a dropped shot he finished the championship, yes you've guessed it, one stroke behind the winner, Tom Watson. Forever known as the 'phantom putt', Irwin felt throughout his career that the moment of madness cost him the British Open title.

## SPOOKED

European Ryder Cup star **Ian Poulter** claimed his rental house was haunted during the Heritage Classic tournament at Hilton Head in April 2011. 'Check this out, we have a ghost in our house this week & I'm not joking we have had some very strange goings on every night,' Poulter said via his Twitter account after Friday's second round. 'No joke for real, very bizarre the door is pretty solid with a dead bolt & number of times it's been unlocked & open… Calling home owner now!' The following day Poulter shot a worst-of-the-week score of 75 to send him crashing out of contention.

## HARD TO SWALLOW

A police investigation was ordered in the Republic of **Ireland** after undertakers found a golf ball lodged in the throat of a deceased south Dublin businessman in 2010! The shocking discovery was made by funeral home staff as they prepared the man's body for burial. The golf ball was found when the undertakers made an incision in the upper chest and neck area during the embalming process. Not found during a previous post-mortem at St James Hospital in Dublin, the unnamed model of ball may have been forced down the man's throat afterwards as a prank. In the coroner's report, foul play was ruled out despite the ball having been lodged in the throat for a significant period of time.

## BANKROLLING GAMES OF GOLF

The Northern Trust Bank of Chicago was criticised by U.S. Government **inspectors** when they discovered how much money it had spent entertaining guests at a golf tournament it sponsored in Los Angeles in February in 2009. The bank was known to have received more than $1.5 billion in a federal bailout package to help them through the recent global downturn. Barney Frank of Massachusetts, Chairman of the House Financial Services Committee, along with seventeen Democrats, demanded they repay the money they had spent on corporate entertainment.

## APROBLEM WITH HOOKING

Twenty-Six **Indonesian** female caddies were arrested for selling sex to golfers at a resort in Kulai, Malaysia. In June 2011, an employee who worked at the usually reputable resort informed the police that the caddies were 'doing a lot more that just carrying the golfers' bags!'

## A BRIDGE TOO FAR

As difficult tee shots go it was in a different league! Even Tiger Woods admitted that it was 'nerve racking' hitting a series of drives down one side of the Bosphorus Bridge in **Istanbul** on 6 November 2013. A publicity stunt arranged prior to the Turkish Airlines Open, half of the six-lane bridge was closed while Woods uniquely hit drives from Europe into Asia. 'I've never done that one before,' he told reporters. 'I've hit balls down airports before on runways but never down a bridge…' Describing it as the narrowest fairway he'd ever seen, he was concerned about hitting cars still allowed to drive down the right-hand side! 'So if I lose any balls to the right, there's an international incident right there,' he said, only half-joking.

## BOHN LUCKY I GUESS

Proving you cannot keep a good man down **Jason** Bohn shot a world-record 58 in the final round of the 2001 Bayer Championship, the last full-field event of the season on the Canadian Professional Golf Association Tour. Bohn, twenty-eight, raced to nine-under over his first seven holes en route to the record-breaking thirteen-under score at Huron Oaks Golf Club. Finishing with a tournament winning four-round total of 260, it was not the first time the former University of Alabama student had made the headlines. In 1992 Bohn won a cool $1 million for a much publicised ace in a charity tournament in Tuscaloosa. Aged just nineteen he funded his pro career with the $5,000 a month he picked up each month for the next twenty years.

## JACK OF CLUBS

Movie legend **Jack Nicholson** found himself in court in February 1994 for threatening another motorist after being cut up in traffic in Los Angeles. Thankfully for the *One Flew Over the Cuckoo's Nest* actor, the judge dismissed assault and vandalism charges against him after he was accused of smashing the motorist's windscreen with a five-iron. Reputedly the gravel-voiced star's only comment was: 'I should have used the driver on the son-of-a-bitch…'

## THE DRAGON'S DEN

The **Jade Dragon** at Lijiang City, China, is officially credited as the longest golf course in the world at an eye-watering 8,450 yards. Even with allowances made for the thin air of the Himalayas, which – at 10,000 ft. (3,050 m) above sea level – allows shots to travel 10 per cent farther, the Jade Dragon is a terrifying prospect for the average golfer with a 735-yd par 5, a 525-yd par 4 and a 270-yd par 3.

## WILD THING GETS WILDER

**John Daly** recorded his first win on American soil in nine years at the Callaway Golf Pebble Beach Invitational in May, 2003. A non-PGA Tour tournament, it proved the trigger for one of the most turbulent periods of his life. In July his wife Sherrie Miller gave birth to a new son, John Patrick Daly II. Then her parents were indicted in Mississippi for their involvement in a million-dollar drug ring and an illegal gambling operation. John was not implicated but the news affected him badly. In his last seven events of the year he missed the cut, withdrew or was disqualified. In addition, his caddie Mike Peterson quit along with John's childhood friend and personal assistant, Donnie Crabtree. No wonder they call the two-time major winner 'Wild Thing'.

## IRISH EYES DEFINITELY NOT SMILING
**Jose-Maria Olazabal** and Padraig Harrington locked horns during the Seve Trophy in November 2003 after the Irishman questioned the Spaniard's decision to repair a pitch mark on the third green in the final day singles. Played at the Campo de Golf Parador El Saler in Spain, Olazabal felt his integrity had been questioned. Adding to the tension Harrington then holed a putt on the final green to halve his match as GB & I ran out winners over Continental Europe 15–13. Face-to-face beside the eighteenth green, Olazabal refused all efforts to mediate including those by team captains Seve Ballesteros and Colin Montgomerie. Dragged away before things got physical, they made up later. Harrington said later: 'It's really not worth losing a friend over.'

## DROPPING IN FOR A GAME OF GOLF
**Japanese** woman Takae Gassho, thirty-eight, from Sapporo, died in a freak accident in 2009 after the turf under her feet collapsed during a round of golf with her husband and two children. Playing on the Le Petaw Golf Club on the Japanese island of Hokkaido, she plunged into a 5m-deep sinkhole. It was blamed on melting spring-time mountain snow flowing just below the surface. A Hokkaido Golf

Association official said that normally golf clubs conducted visual check-ups every day but no one noticed that a hollow space was forming underground.

## CADDIE CAN'T COUNT

Spanish professional **Jose Manuel Lara** was disqualified from the BMW International Open at Gut Larchenhof in Cologne, Germany, on 21 June 2012. Playing the second hole in the opening round, caddie Mathias Vinson discovered he had fifteen clubs in his bag. Knowing that it meant at least four penalty shots for his employer, the Argentine bagman attempted to hide the extra club in thick bushes by the green. But his actions were spotted by Lara's playing partners Damien McGrane and Peter Hedblom, who became suspicious. When challenged, the caddie admitted there had been fifteen clubs in the bag. John Paramor, Chief referee of the European Tour, said: 'We are satisfied [Lara] had no knowledge of what was going on.' But a golfer is responsible for the actions of his caddie, so out he went.

## THE COMEBACK KING

Dustin **Johnson** announced his surprise departure from the PGA Tour on 31 July 2014, citing 'personal challenges'. The decision meant the thirty-year-old big-hitting star missed the Ryder Cup scheduled for Gleneagles in Scotland in October. Fourth on the United States FedEx Cup points list at the time the American was considered one of the favourites for the PGA Championship scheduled for the following week at Valhalla Golf Club in Louisville, Kentucky.

Instead his career seemed in ruins, especially after *Golf* magazine in the U.S. reported that Johnson had failed three drug tests: one for marijuana in 2009 and two for cocaine, in 2012 and 2014. PGA Tour officials responded by saying that Johnson was taking voluntary leave and was not under suspension for drug abuse. Johnson was equally adamant that it was nothing more than a career readjustment, saying: 'By committing the time and resources necessary to improve my mental health, physical well-being and emotional foundation, I am confident that I will be better equipped to fulfil my potential and become a consistent champion.' It proved the right decision. In September his fiancee Paulina Gretzky, daughter of ice hockey legend Wayne Gretzky, announced that she was pregnant with the couple's first child. Proving a real turning point Johnson returned to the game in February 2015 a fitter and much wiser individual winning the WGC-Cadillac Championship followed by a second place finish in the U.S. Open in June.

## CADDIE WARS

LPGA star Jessica **Korda** fired her caddie midway through the third round of the United States Women's Open. Played at Sebonack Golf Club on Long Island on 29 June 2013, the twenty-year-old American professional turned to her boyfriend Johnny DelPrete who was following in the gallery and said, 'Grab the bag, let's go.' Korda later told reporters that she and bagman Jason Gilroyed had several disagreements over the first nine holes. 'It's a U.S. Open!' she said. 'It's a big week for me… I was just not in the right state of mind.' Thankfully, the switch seemed to work: after shooting 5 over on the front nine, Korda was 1 under par the remainder of the round. Finishing with a 76 she ended the round tied for sixth at 1 over, 11 strokes behind leader Inbee Park, who went on to win.

## BETTER LATE THAN NEVER

Two spectators were killed by lightning, and five others injured including professional Horton Smith, in the **Kansas City Open** on 6 June 1937. The bolt struck near the ninth green of the Hillcrest Country Club. Six weeks later the U.S. Golf Association issued guidelines on 'how to act in a thunderstorm' to its entire list of member clubs.

## WAYWARD DRIVE

**Kansas City Open** story two; in 1959 the final-round pairing of Don Fairfield and Bob Goalby were putting out on the final hole at Blue Hills Country Club when an unmanned motor car came crashing down the hill after its hand brake failed. With the crowd three deep, it was lucky that only a handful of people were injured including a man who ended up pinned against a tree. 'All of a sudden we hear all this noise,' recalled Fairfield. 'I look over and here comes this car behind the green and to the left coming down the hill, and it's hitting people like bowling pins, knocking them down.. It was chaos.' After order had been restored and the victims treated, Fairfield made the difficult decision to putt out and not surprisingly, he missed. Tied with Dow Finsterwald, officials made the extraordinary decision to hold a play-off down the par 4 first hole a few minutes later! Still visibly shaken, Fairfield could not match his opponent's birdie and failed to register what would have been his second win on Tour. 'I went to my locker, cleaned it out, got in my car and started driving to Dallas,' he said. 'I was so upset I didn't sleep that night.'

## A KLASS APART

Beverly **Klass** quit the LPGA Tour in 1988 after suffering a debilitating spell of the putting yips. Born in Encino, California, in 1957, she was considered the ultimate golf prodigy. Receiving her first set of clubs aged three, she won a National Pee Wee event by 65 strokes just over twelve months later! Dominating junior tournaments for the next few years, she proved so good that she was actually banned from competing. Her pushy father Jack then announced to the press that Beverly would turn pro and play on the LPGA Tour in 1967 – she was aged just ten! Using a cut-down, 25-inch driver, she competed in four tournaments including the U.S. Women's Open where she set a record as the youngest player to ever compete at the age of 10 years, 7 months, and 21 days. Facing a storm of criticism the LPGA was forced to re-write its eligibility rules, bringing in a minimum playing age of eighteen. Jack Klass then decided to sue the LPGA. A settlement was eventually reached but the decision stood and young Beverly's career was cut short aged just eleven. Not that it stopped him from exploiting his daughter's talents. When she was 15, Jack checked her out of a sanatorium in Camarillo, CA where she had been sent after refusing to go home. He then flew her to Tokyo for an exhibition match against the Japanese star Chako Higuchi with barely any rest. In 1976, Beverly qualified for the LPGA Tour but she was not the smiling, happy-go-lucky girl who regularly launched the ball well over 230 yards. Her form was inconsistent. In twelve full seasons, her best finishes were tied second in both the 1984 West Virginia Classic and San Jose Classic. Preferring the less cut-throat world of amateur golf she won twenty-five events around the Los Angeles area. Her father died in 1981.

## A HAZARDOUS GAME

The day before the 2008 Casio World Open was due to be played at the **Kuroshio Country Club in Kochi, Japan**, a local newspaper received an anonymous phone call saying that anti-personnel mines had been buried all over the course! Following a series of small explosions that knocked out windows in the clubhouse and in the corporate sponsor

building, organisers had to make the difficult decision whether to go ahead or not. Police checked the venue for about two hours following the call but found nothing. Deploying around 160 officers at the course and hotel where the players were staying, the tournament went ahead without further incident.

## THE RELUCTANT GOLFER

United States President John F. **Kennedy** permitted himself to be photographed on a golf course for the first time in 1961. Joined by his father, Joseph P. Kennedy and brothers-in-law, Stephen E. Smith and Peter Lawford, on his home course in Hyannisport, he was very conscious how it would look to the wider country. Consequently, the President declined to pose with a club in his hands and reporters were allowed to witness only the first drive. 'Kennedy approaches golf with enthusiasm but without dedication,' said a report in *Time* magazine. 'He plays swiftly, rarely pausing to ponder a shot. He almost never completes a full 18-hole round, generally packing up his clubs after 9 or 11. Much of his pleasure comes from wagering on himself...'

## TEED OFF!

William **Lowell** was granted a patent for a revolutionary new golf tee in 1925. Following an unsuccessful attempt to make them from gutta-percha, which proved too brittle, the New York dentist turned to wood and plastic in the early 1920s. Originally painted green he quickly changed to an ivory colour with a red top so that they could be seen more easily. The so-called 'Reddy Tee' comprised a narrow cone topped with a saucer-like platform similar to the shape in widespread use today. In 1922 Lowell hired two professional golfers, Walter Hagen and Joe Kirkwood, to use his product in all their exhibition matches. They proved so popular that after they hit, spectators would scramble to retrieve them. If they were broken, fans would take them

home and glue them together! Inspiring other tee makers to copy his design, Lowell lost his patent after a long legal battle to defend his copyright.

## COME BACK LATER

Ever wondered what happens to that ball you hit into the middle of a forest? According to a 2014 report by the Danish Golf Association **lost golf balls** are taking between 100 and 1,000 years to decompose naturally. As feathery golf balls from the early 1800s can sell for £5,000-plus at golf memorabilia auctions, someone in the next millennium could be in for a windfall.

## CHOPPER POWER

An unusual experiment took place at the **Locust Grove Club Links** in Rahway, New Jersey on 25 June 1931. In an effort to demonstrate the flexibility of the Kelett Auto Giro – a type of early one-man helicopter – an unnamed golfer flew from hole to hole in an 18-hole match. Avoiding trees, hills, ditches etc. the 'windmill-plane' was parked by the side of each green and managed to negotiate the round in safety.

## THE PERFECT PLAYING PARTNER

**London golfing circles** were rocked in autumn 1928 by the forced resignation of two members of a so-called 'leading golf club' on a charge of cheating. In November, The *Weekly Dispatch* reported how suspicions had been aroused when one or the other would always win club competitions whenever they played together. They were unable to reproduce the same form in matches with other members. The committee hired a private detective! 'Dressed in golfing garb' he would watch them from a distance using trees and foliage as cover. As before, one of them returned the winning score. Afterwards, the private eye reported how they had improved their lies and not declared the correct amount of strokes taken. Calling an emergency committee meeting the following day, the club captain interviewed them privately and insisted they resign their membership with immediate effect!

## BRAVEHEART MANGRUM

**Lloyd Mangrum** faced Byron Nelson and Vic Ghezzi in a play-off for the 1946 U.S. Open at Canterbury Golf Club in Beachwood, Ohio. Tied after a four-round score of 284 (-4) the three went into an eighteen-hole playoff the next morning where they all shot par 72s. Forced into another eighteen holes that afternoon, a thunderstorm rumbled overhead. Unlike today when lightning suspends play, the three pros were told to continue. The danger unnerved both Ghezzi and Nelson but appeared to calm ex-Army man Mangrum. As journalist Oscar Fraley observed: 'The former corporal was just another G.I. again for a minute. His cream-colored sports shirt seemed to turn to khaki and to him it no longer was a golf course. That rumble was too familiar and it meant trouble. And that's when Mangrum looked up at the flashes, laughed and really started to play.' Mangrum made three birdies over the final six holes including a clutch 7-foot par putt on the final green. Scoring a par 72, he beat his rivals by a stroke each. 'It was the greatest demonstration of courage I ever saw on a golf course,' commented two-time Amateur Champion Bud Ward.

## THE BIG BANG THEORY

Looking for a **lost ball** near the eighth fairway of the Augusta Municipal Golf Course in Georgia in 2009, a golfer found more than he bargained for when he unearthed a half-buried hand grenade! Recent heavy rains had unearthed the wartime relic and after a nervous wait for the bomb squad the so-called 'pineapple' grenade was safely detonated. The golf course was built over land that was formerly part of Camp Hancock, a sprawling U.S. Army base in World War I.

## LOCKED OUT!

Bobby **Locke** won the British Open at Royal Lytham in July 1952 despite a dramatic start to the final day when he became separated from his golf clubs! Looking to overhaul a four-stroke lead held by 1947 champion Fred Daly, he discovered the private garage his car was in was securely locked. Not usually a problem, except that his golf clubs were locked in the car boot. With two rounds to play and a tee-off time of 8.50am, a local milkman came to his aid by offering him a lift in his milk van to obtain the keys from the garage owner who lived a short distance away. Locke duly retrieved the keys and only made it to the first tee with a few minutes to spare. Even with no practice shots, the South African star produced two good rounds of 74 and 73 to beat Peter Thomson by a single stroke. He was the only player to finish under par for the week. It was considered a controversial victory after a number of fellow pros complained about how much time Locke took to play each shot. During the third round for example, he lost three holes on the group in front and Norman Von Nida, playing in the match behind, lodged a formal complaint. Before the final round Locke was issued with a warning, but he blamed the inadequate crowd control and the matter was dismissed. Interestingly, the time he took to finish the third round was three-and-a-half hours, which would be considered a gallop today!

## NAKED AMBITION

The only naturist golf course in Europe opened in 1992 just west of Bordeaux on France's Atlantic coast. **'La Jenny'** is one of the few places in the world which caters exclusively for golfers who prefer to play *au naturel*. It even has its own club professional and stages numerous tournaments throughout the year. Part of the France 4 Naturisme group of sites, it has a 'nudity is obligatory' rule, and the only time it does not enforce its nudity clause is during inclement weather.

## ANGOLA NINE-HOLER

Once known as the 'bloodiest prison in America' **Louisiana State Penitentiary** in the United States opened a new nine-hole golf course in 2003. Situated on the banks of the Mississippi River, golfers putt out barely a good eight-iron from the razor-wire-topped fences and guard towers... The

brainchild of Chief Warden Burl Cain, it is appropriately named Prison View Golf Course. Built on an old cow pasture, it was constructed by the inmates as part of a reward system. None of the 5,108 prisoners can play it but many of the less dangerous ones can earn credits by cutting the grass. Open to prison employees and local townspeople, any 'unknown' visitor requesting a green fee must submit to an extensive background check. Convicted felons and prison visitors need not apply. Green fees are $10 for nine holes, which has to be the bargain of the century considering the unique location. The opening hole has a raised tee where golfers climb up fifty steps. Offering a sweeping view of the entire prison it also doubles up as a vantage point should anyone go 'walkabout'. The tee on the seventh is close enough to hear comments from the worst-of-the-worst in Camp J – many of whom will never be free again. While the ninth green is close to the prison kennels, which house malamute tracking dog hybrids that have been bred out of a wolf! The course logo is a set of handcuffs, welded shut.

## FOR THE LOVE OF GOLF

**Lee Hae-chan** is a former Prime Minister of South Korea. A member of the liberal Uri Party, he took office in 2004 but was forced to resign less than two years later in 2006 amidst the so-called 'Golf Game Scandal'. He was discovered playing golf on the day when a nationwide strike of railway workers began and the editor of the influential *JoongAng Daily* newspaper ran a story questioning his 'love of the people'. Expected to take command of the situation and mediate the strike, Chan was playing golf at Busan with a group of local businessmen – one of whom was found to have a criminal record. Worse still, the day was a sacred public holiday to mark a 1919 mass uprising for independence against Japanese colonial rule! A few days later an editorial read: 'Mr Lee is going too far to say that he was playing golf as a hobby. Immediately before showing respect to the dead in September 2004 after an accidental shooting in the nation's military, Mr Lee was criticised for playing golf. When a forest fire broke out in Gangwon province in April last year and the nation's southern regions were suffering from flood damage in July, he was also playing golf…'

## A DIFFERENT TYPE OF SHOT!

In the days leading up to the 2006 Masters at Augusta National a rental car driven by golf pro Tom **Lehman** was shot at. On 5 April, he drove to the local airport to pick up his son. The former British Open champion told police how he was approaching the off-ramp of the Bobby Jones Expressway when he heard a large explosion. A shot had been fired from a passing car and the bullet had penetrated the rear driver-side door of his sports utility vehicle. 'It was a surreal experience,' said Lehman. 'I got to the airport and there was a bullet in the car.' Lehman was not injured and police later arrested a suspect on felony charges.

## MIND GAMES

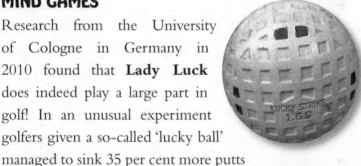

Research from the University of Cologne in Germany in 2010 found that **Lady Luck** does indeed play a large part in golf! In an unusual experiment golfers given a so-called 'lucky ball' managed to sink 35 per cent more putts than those who were playing with a normal ball! In a so-called 'blind' test those with the lucky ball sank 6.4 putts out of 10, nearly two more putts on average than the others.

## SWATTING DRIVES AWAY

At the RE/MAX World **Long Drive Championship** at Mesquite Regional Park in Nevada in 2008, controversy ensued after the Women's Division was won by someone who was previously a male cop. Lana Lawless won with drives ranging from 308 yards down to 245 yards into a 40 mph headwind, but afterwards she was forced to defend her right to compete in the event: 'This is who I am. This is my life!' she said. 'That other person, that 254-pound SWAT cop I used to be, he's gone. He's not coming back.' Unfortunately her win was not popular with other competitors, such as former world champion Lee Brandon: 'In 2005, the USGA approved transgender involvement in competition. So I don't see how we can dispute this. However, if a woman has the knees, hands and feet of a man, she has genetic real estate that is more gifted.'

## MONEY MAKES MONEY

A so-called **'Match of the Century'** was played over 21-22 March 1926 at two different California courses. Unable to agree on the sale of Chicago property worth more than half a million dollars, Frederick H. Bartlett and Archie M. Andrews agreed to play for the difference of $25,000 in their valuations. Watched by a large crowd at both the Midwick Country Club and Annandale Golf Club, Andrews won, forcing Bartlett to pay $575,000 for the Chicago property instead of $550,000 if Bartlett had won – the equivalent of many tens of millions today.

## MACK THE SLICE

A **mysterious masked** golfer announced that he was

going to play the 'longest golf course in the world!'
According to the Sydney Sun newspaper he would hit
a golf ball from Brisbane to Adelaide in Australia in May
1931 – a distance of 1,800 miles. Going under the name
of 'Mr Rex Mack' he told reporters that he would play
golf at the rate of ten miles a day, including a number
of rest periods. Publicising his world record attempt, he
arrived in Sydney in April and played through the city.
He estimated that his 'round' would take about eight
months to complete, with his final shots taken in Adelaide
in January 1932. He would carry a complete set of clubs
but use just his putter in populated areas in order to
avoid being a danger to the public! A motor car would
accompany him throughout the journey and pick up a
new scorecard marker each day from towns on the way in
order to ensure fair play. The only rule was that the ball
must not be moved from any lie. To finance the trip he
would appear at local shows and fairs in his capacity as a
'celebrity'. In the end the original 'course' was replaced
by a much shorter one of 700 miles between Brisbane and
Sydney. According to one report, he finished his 'round' in
April 1932, took approximately 25,000 strokes and lost 57
balls in total. Along the way he 'putted' through a private
zoo including replaying one shot that had landed inside a
leopard's cage! Apart from thirst and exhaustion, the most
difficult section of the trip was through a wild stretch
of bush country between Woodburn and Chatsworth
in New South Wales. At one point the ball came to rest
beside a large brown snake. Fortunately for him, it had

been dead for some time and he completed his journey without further incident.

## LOCATION, LOCATION, LOCATION?

The last place on earth you would build a new golf course is near the base of an active volcano. But that was the decision made by the owners of the **Merapi Golf Club** in Indonesia in 2003. Located just five miles from the actual crater, Merapi means 'Mountain of Fire' and already boasts over a dozen eruptions, including some which resulted in human fatalities. Considered to be among the most active geological regions on the planet, it is not far from the infamous volcanic island of Krakatoa, which killed over 35,000 people in 1883.

## CROC SHOCK!

A fifty-year-old American golfer vacationing in **Mexico** endured an almost fatal attack by a crocodile at the Iberostar Cancun Golf Club in July 2013. Edward Lunger, a 15 handicap, from Holtsville, Long Island described how he hooked his ball into a bunker where an angry female croc jumped out of nearby bushes before pulling him to the ground by his hand. Grabbing a boulder and smashing the reptile on the head, one of his playing partners helped set him free but Mr Lunger still lost two fingers in the attack. 'She pulled me back and flipped me, and I went to the ground,' Lunger recalled. 'I couldn't feel my hand. It was like my whole body was on fire.' Adding insult to injury he was rushed to a local hospital but forced to pay the $17,800 bill up front before he could get treatment. Splitting the cost on their credit cards, Lunger and his golfing buddies then filed a $2.25 million law suit for negligence against the hotel owners. Fought out in a Brooklyn Federal Court in September, Lunger claimed there were no warnings of rampaging reptiles. He later found the crocs had been introduced to the golf course, in his lawyer's opinion, 'as a marketing tourist attraction and hence profit-enhancing lure.' During his recovery Lunger also accused club officials of pressuring him to sign papers absolving the resort of any responsibility. When he refused, they alleged that he had prompted the attack by enticing the crocodile out of the water with chicken. 'We came with nothing,' said Lunger's friend Mark Martin. 'We rented the clubs there. We [bought] the balls there. Where would we be getting chicken?'

## BAVARIAN GOLF BULL PROBLEMS
A German farmer filed a negligence lawsuit in 1994 against the owners of a golf club near **Munich** for 'murdering' thirty of his cows. He filed the suit after a veterinarian investigating the mysterious death of one of his animals found a golf ball lodged in its throat. Further investigation found approximately 2,000 golf balls lodged in the stomachs of his unfortunate herd.

## WHAT HAPPENED TO WINDMILLS ON MINI GOLF COURSES?
The **'Mission Impossi-Hole'** is part of a futuristic 'Smash Putt' putting course in Portland, Oregon. An alternative golf experience hosted in the city through to the end of March

2015, the hi-tech hole is a salute to the Mission Impossible movie franchise. Set in a futuristic cage with lasers zigzagging all around it, an alarm sounds and a 'one-stroke penalty' sign starts flashing when one of the laser beams is crossed!

## COURSE FIT FOR A KING

The **Maharaja of Cooch Behar** employed American professional Ross Sobel to teach him the game of golf and help construct a private course at his home in the Indian state of West Bengal in 1920. Educated at Edinburgh University, his Royal Highness Jitendra Narayan Bhup Bahadur had developed an interest in the game and wanted his own links course within the confines of the Cooch Behar Palace, which coincidentally bore more than a passing resemblance to Buckingham Palace in London. He had a reputation for being incredibly vain and knowing this, Sobel designed a nine-hole course without a single hazard! Not only were there no bunkers, the actual hole was double the normal size to facilitate better putting. The fairways of the 2,800 yard course were also unusually wide. Known to be erratic off the tee, the Maharajah never actually walked a step. Instead he rode in a howdah on an elephant with a retinue of servants marching in front and behind. Those in front located his ball while those behind were armed with rakes and spades to smooth out the divots the elephant made! Sadly, golf in this remote Indian state was short-lived. After the Maharaja died on 20 December 1922, the course fell into disrepair and no trace of it now exists.

## MYSTERIOUS MONTY – OR SHOULD THAT BE LAVERNE?

Sportswriter Grantland Rice caused a major stir in U.S. golfing circles when he wrote in the January 1936 edition of *The American Golfer* magazine how: 'The U.S. Amateur champion of 1936, whoever it was, would not be the best amateur in the country because John **Montague** was not entered!' Up to that point, no one had heard of 'Monty' other than a select few from Lakeview Golf Club in California where he was a member. A notorious gambler, he had beaten low handicap Bing Crosby using just a garden spade and a billiards cue! Friend and golfing buddy to stars like Oliver Hardy, he regularly blasted the ball in excess of 300 yards. Rarely shooting more than 70, he had refused all offers to play golf 'officially' or turn professional. 'I have played several rounds with John Montagu (sic) in California and I'll take him as an even bet against any golfer you can name,' wrote Rice. Unbeknown to him or anyone else, there was a reason 'Mysterious Monty' kept away from the public eye. Under his real name of Laverne Moore he had fled to California after a botched bank robbery for which he was later arrested and tried. Despite being found not guilty, his reputation among the Hollywood elite was gone forever and he ended his days in poverty.

## BLOW HARD

A **mini riot** caused the cancellation of an LPGA tournament in Gyeongju in South Korea in October 2007. Over 500 spectators attending the Hana Bank-Kolon Championship in North Gyeongsang Province menaced officials and threw water bottles for almost an hour after play was suspended for a third day because of strong winds. They demanded a refund of their entrance fees and transportation costs. One spectator threatened a foreign golfer who had come out to sign autographs. Fearing for the player's safety, the tournament organisers called it off with many of the professionals heading quickly for the airport.

## A QUICK EXIT

Former Al Capone henchman **'Machine Gun' McGurn** attempted to qualify for the 1933 Western Open at Olympia Fields near Chicago. A talented golfer, McGurn was reputedly one-under-par through six holes. Tipped off that cops awaited him on the eighteenth green, he hurriedly picked up his ball and left the course, leaving the cops empty-handed. The tournament was won by MacDonald Smith.

## THEY SHOOT GOLFERS DON'T THEY?

A **marathon** stamina-sapping 108-hole tournament took place at Fenway Golf Club in White Plains, New York from 24 to 27 September 1939. Playing for total prize money of \$13,500, additional cash prizes were also on offer for the longest drive and best approach shot each day at the Westchester Open. Reflecting an era when long, drawn-out events like 'danceathon' competitions were in vogue, the six-round tourney was a test of endurance as well as skill. Hoping the new format would replace the standard 72-hole tournament, the organisers also made the slightly dotty decision to highlight each hole position with two concentric chalk circles! The idea was to make it more interesting for the fans but by the end of six rounds, the almost indelible circles made each green look like a target range. Not that it bothered Sam Snead, who won the \$5,000 first prize with scores of 73, 72, 73, 72, 71 and 69.

## DON'T THREATEN A HERO

Lloyd **Mangrum** won the St Paul Open in 1951 despite a death threat the night before the final round. Receiving a telephone call telling him to lose, police surmised it came from the same gamblers who also called Sam Snead saying: 'We have a big money bet. Now you get in there and start playing. We don't want Mangrum to win.' Accompanied by two policemen all the way around, the Second World War Purple Heart winner dismissed it as nonsense and played well enough for a clear victory.

## MARKS FOR EFFORT

Legendary comic Harpo **Marx** set out to complete an unusual world record at the newly opened Tamarisk Country Club in Palm Springs, California in 1952. With

August temperatures soaring above 110 degrees, the legendary funny man drove his buggy to a nearby par 3 with a couple of clubs and fifty balls. It was late in the evening and the course was deserted. Taking one last look around, he stripped naked before teeing up the first of fifty tee-shots! 'I was determined to be a famous first,' he wrote in his autobiography years later, 'The first naked man in history to fire a hole-in-one! I didn't make it but I came damn close. I came within six inches, to be exact, of immortality.' Not that he was in danger of being thrown off as he part-owned the club with showbiz pals George Burns, Jack Benny and Danny Kaye, among others.

## DOG LEGS

Two employees at **Moanalua Golf Club** in Hawaii were charged with stealing a member's pet dog before killing it and eating it. Witnesses told officials they saw Saturnino Palting, fifty-eight, and Nelson Domingo, forty-three, put the dog named Caddy into a car and drive away at the end of their shift on 16 December 2007. The dog's owner, Frank Manuma, said he tied up the eight-month-old German Shepherd while he played a round of golf but the dog was gone when he came back. The club fired the workers and investigators later told how they had butchered and eaten the pet. Both men were later indicted on theft and animal cruelty charges.

## GOODBYE NORMA JEANE

Joe DiMaggio purchased a set of golf clubs for his new bride, **Marilyn Monroe**, shortly after they got married on 14 January 1954. 'She hits a long ball when she hits it,' he told reporters after they returned from their honeymoon in Japan. Proving that golf is not a recipe for a happy union, the marriage lasted just 274 days.

## SOUTH POLE SMASH

A measured drive of 2,640 yards was achieved by an Australian **meteorologist** Nils Lied over an ice field near the Mawson Base Camp in Antarctica in 1961.

## BRING BACK MY BALL!

Legendary golfer Byron **Nelson** (see photo, page 118) finished fourth in the Hershey Open in September to collect $450 prize money. It would have been more had he located a lost ball in the final round after a wayward drive cost him two strokes and outright second-place prize money of $750. A few weeks later Nelson received an anonymous letter from a well-wisher describing how, 'a lady in our party, one of my guests, unwittingly picked up your ball. She knows nothing about the game and did not realise what a lost ball means to a player. I did not learn about it until it was too late…' As he turned the page, three $100 money orders fell onto the floor by way of compensation! 'You could have knocked me over with a wooden tee,' said Nelson.

## GOLF GOES NUCLEAR

Bart Leiper of Gatlinburg, Tennessee, was looking for a unique way of publicising the opening of a new public golf course in 1955. Working for the local Chamber of Commerce, he considered releasing 1,000 pigeons on the first tee of the aptly named Pigeon Forge Golf Club but could not guarantee their return. Then he hit upon a brilliant idea of **'nuclear'** powered golf balls! Visiting an Atomic Energy facility at nearby Oak Ridge National Laboratory, he persuaded a scientist to inject three golf balls with pellets of radioactive cobalt 60. He then headed home to Gatlinburg with them in his car. A few days later he had a swim-suited Miss Gatlinburg posing by the clubhouse with the golf balls in her gloved hand while photographers were invited to take photos from, 'a safe distance.' Adding to the drama, he employed a blindfolded caddy to demonstrate that a radioactive golf ball could be found no matter how deep the rough. Driving them off the first, he used a borrowed Geiger counter to locate them even though one had found the trees. Bart was then asked if such balls could put golf equipment manufacturers out of business. Explaining the atomic golf ball was still only an experiment, he said that even if the Atomic Energy Commission approved their manufacture, radioactive golf balls would probably cost $20 to $35 each. 'And who would pay that?' he asked.

## A RELUCTANT GOLFER

By the time Richard **Nixon's** second term as U.S. President ended in scandal in August 1974, he had little time for golf.

Dealing with the Vietnam War and Watergate crisis, 'Tricky Dicky' had originally taken up golf as a way of spending more time with President Dwight D. Eisenhower after he appointed him Vice President in 1956. Arnold Palmer once said: 'It probably wouldn't have sat well with the parents of those young people to know the commander-in-chief had taken the afternoon off to beat a ball around Congressional or Burning Tree.' After leaving office, Nixon retired to his home in California where friends built him a three-hole course. Sadly, the joys of golf were still lost on him. 'By the time you get dressed, drive out there, play eighteen holes and come home, you've blown seven hours,' he said. 'There are better things you can do with your time.'

## AS COOL AS ICE

A member of the **New York Rangers** ice hockey team struck a drive from the top of Mount Edith Cavell in 1955. Landing on the Ghost Glacier below at a distance of 5,000 feet it rolled another 1,000 feet before coming to a halt on a rocky ledge. Writing to the Royal and Ancient Golf Club of St Andrews he asked whether or not it qualified as the longest drive ever hit? Not surprisingly, his claim to have hit a 2,000-yard drive was quickly dismissed.

## AVOID THE ROUGH AND BRING A HELICOPTER

The world's longest golf course opened in the desolate Australian Outback at **Nullarbor Plains** in October 2009. Offering a gentle 842-mile stroll through some of the most inhospitable terrain found on the planet, the average round on Nullarbor Links takes about four days! Starting at the mining town of Kalgoorlie in Western Australia and finishing at Ceduna in the state of South Australia, the par 71 layout includes holes borrowed from existing golf courses with others built from scratch to link them up. Using a motor car instead of a golf buggy to travel along the desolate Eyre Highway, the actual holes are of average size but the distances in between often amount to hundreds of miles. Played in temperatures over 40 degrees in the Australian summer, anyone who finishes (or should that be survives?) is presented with a certificate saying: 'You have played the World's Longest Golf Course.' Aimed at the new breed of 'extreme' golfer, Nullarbor Links is not expected to attract many senior citizen events.

## TALK ABOUT A SHOTGUN START!

A **Nevada** man grabbed a gun and shot a golfer who hit a golf ball through his bedroom window in September 2012. According to the police report, Jeff Fleming was woken up after a ball smashed through the window of his house, which bordered the Lakeridge Golf Course in Reno. He responded by firing a shotgun at the errant golfer who had dropped another ball and was about to hit again! Fleming's lawyer, Larry Dunn, said his client was only trying to scare the golfer who only realised that he had been hit in his arm and legs after he stopped running. With no previous criminal record, Fleming faced up to ten years in jail after pleading guilty to a felony charge of battery with a deadly weapon but was let off with five years' probation along with a severe warning about his future conduct.

## BELGIAN BIG HITTER

**Nicolas Colsaerts** hit the longest drive ever recorded on the European Tour in the first round of the Wales Open at Celtic Manor on 18 September 2014. The Belgian pro hit his tee shot 447 yards on the par-five eighteenth hole of the Twenty-Ten course, which hosted the 2010 Ryder Cup. He took full advantage of a prevailing breeze and the hard condition of the fairway at the 575-yard hole, which Colsaerts was playing as his ninth. Colsearts' drive was five yards longer than the previous known European Tour mark of 442 yards set by India's Shiv Kapur in the third round of the 2012 Madeira Islands Open. He went on to make an eagle on the hole.

## NET GAIN

A **New Jersey man** received a $725,000 settlement after a golf-related accident left him with a damaged cornea. Thomas Guhl was driving in Farmingdale, New York, when a golf ball smashed into his windshield in 2006. Guhl alleged the ball had been struck from nearby Eagle Oaks Golf and Country Club and was launched toward his car by a mower. Because no protective netting was in evidence to prevent balls from leaving the course, the court found in his favour.

## SLOW PLAY LEADS TO DISASTER

**Nicholas Jay Shampine** was arrested on a charge of second-degree assault after a confrontation between two groups on the fourteenth green of the Auburn Golf Course in July 2008 ended in violence. The victim, forty-five-year-old James Compton, was in the group in front when an argument broke out after Compton was accused of slow play. Allegedly having grabbed Shampine's brother, he was struck on the head by a 6-iron. Compton was airlifted to Harborview Medical Center after the attack, which left him with permanent brain damage and memory loss. Shampine was found guilty and was required to serve between eighteen and thirty-six months in community custody as part of his sentence.

## NA TANKS

Kevin **Na** recorded the worst score on a par-four hole in PGA Tour history in the opening round of the Valero Texas Open on 14 April 2011. The duodecuple bogey 16 came on the par 4 ninth of the Oaks Course at TPC San Antonio where he dropped twelve shots in one hole. The South Korean-born professional later admitted that he had lost count of how many shots he had taken after two wild drives, an unplayable lie and a two-stroke penalty after his ball hit a tree and rebounded onto him. (He admitted taking fifteen strokes but it was later upped by one after a television review).

## SING WHEN YOU'RE WINNING

**Opera** singer Orville Harold and lawyer John Walsh played an unusual match at the Wee Burn Country Club in Darien, Connecticut, in 1927. Wagering $200 on the result, the performer was allowed to sing out two high Cs during the match to compensate for his opponent's lower handicap. Unfortunately, any hope he had of winning was lost when Walsh secretly wore earplugs throughout the entire match.

## UNIVERSITY CHALLENGE

Widespread condemnation followed the **Oxford-Cambridge** University match at Royal Liverpool in Hoylake in May 1930 after the two captains introduced their own local rules on the water-logged course. Agreeing that

both teams should be able to pick out of flooded bunkers without penalty, they were stunned by the vitriolic flood of criticism that met with their decision to alter the accepted rules of the game. Oxford won 12 matches to 3 but Bernard Darwin, golf correspondent of *The Times*, suggested they would be doing the world a service by giving up the game altogether! While a Hoylake member said: 'The Varsities should have been given the opportunity of going elsewhere, if they so desired. Some attempt should have been made to get rid of the water which would have been a simple matter if a pump had been brought into operation. An old fire engine would have performed the work in the space of a few hours.'

## BANK REFUSES A LOAN TO THE PRESIDENT

President Dwight Eisenhower invited Francis **Ouimet** to come to Palm Springs, California and play golf as his guest in the mid-1950s. At the time, the legendary 1913 U.S. Open champion was working in the Boston office of Brown Brothers Harriman, the oldest private bank in the United States. Amazingly, company head Louis Curtis refused Ouimet's request for time off saying somewhat peevishly: 'I do not recall the firm doing any business with the President of the United States!' Hearing about the snub, Eisenhower immediately sent Air Force One to Boston to pick him up! Later, when Ouimet was made the first American-born captain of the R&A, it was Eisenhower who commissioned a painting of Ouimet in his red club jacket. As for BBH, they later named their most private boardroom the Francis Ouimet Room.

## HOW TOUGH IS GOLF ANYWAY?

Rob **O'Neill**, the U.S. Navy SEAL who shot and killed terrorist leader Osama Bin Laden during a dramatic raid on his compound in Pakistan in 2011, announced in 2014 that he had taken up golf as a way of getting over his post-traumatic stress. Sadly it proved the wrong choice. 'The last psychiatrist I spoke to recommended golfing to relieve stress (but) that's a bad idea,' admitted O'Neill in an interview with the *New York Post*: 'Golf's more stressful than combat!'

## LODGING A COMPLAINT

A golfer playing the **Protrero Country Club** in Los Angeles struck a small plane in June 1928 as it was preparing to land on an adjacent runway. Playing his approach to the third green, the loud bang was enough to put the pilot off his approach and he wheeled away from the runway fearing he had struck a bird. He landed safely some distance away with the ball still lodged in the fabric fuselage, but the golfer who struck the ball complained bitterly that he should not have to take a penalty for a theoretical out-of-bounds. Forgetting that he had almost caused a fatal crash, he then wrote to the USGA for a definitive ruling. A short time later they wrote back agreeing, quoting Rule 17 which stated: 'If a ball lodge in anything moving, a ball shall be dropped, or, if on the putting green, placed, as near as possible to where the object was when the ball lodged in it, without penalty.'

## SHOULD HAVE GONE FISHING

American club pro Ray Ainsley stubbornly refused to take a **penalty** drop from a stream guarding the par 5 sixteenth green in the second round of the 1937 U.S. Open at Cherry Hills. After splashing around like a manic dolphin, he eventually made it to the putting surface where he one-putted for a 19 and a championship record highest score! Boasting about the amount of fish he had killed, he was not surprised to hear that he had missed the cut.

## EAT HEALTHY TO PLAY BETTER GOLF, RIGHT?

Gary **Player** praised the nutritive values of raisins in a magazine interview in 1964. Discussing the importance of food in the modern game, Jack Nicklaus admitted that he loved eating as many as six dozen oysters at a sitting, while Billy Casper lived off a diet of buffalo steak and moose burger! Al Geiberger announced that he owed his recent PGA success to peanut-butter-and-jelly sandwiches. 'If I don't eat I get nervous and when I get nervous I make bad decisions,' said Geiberger. 'And the swell thing about peanut butter and jelly is if you forget and leave them in your golf bag, you can still eat them the next day. You can't do that with egg…'

## RYDER CUP TRASH TALK

European Ryder Cup professional **Paul Casey** admitting getting 'professional help' from a councillor in the aftermath of his inflammatory remarks about American Ryder Cup players in 2005. Casey, who played collegiate golf at Arizona State, has an American girlfriend, an American coach in Peter Kostis and still lives in Scottsdale, AZ, caused massive controversy in November 2004 when he said in an interview with *The Sunday Times* that he had learned to 'properly hate' the American team during the recent Ryder Cup in Detroit. 'Oh, we properly hate them,' he was quoted as saying. 'Americans can be bloody annoying. Sometimes they infuriate me. In Scottsdale it's not so bad because the people there have travelled and you can have civilised conversations with them. But the vast majority of Americans simply don't know what is going on.' Dropped by Titleist, one of his sponsors, Casey said: 'I don't think anyone has been more affected and upset than I have. The hurt I've caused will live with me as a huge source of regret for the rest of my life.'

## AVOID THE BUNKERS IF YOU CAN

A party of **Pittsburgh** golfers from Oakmont Country Club inaugurated a new game of 'Beach Golf' in March 1912. At low tide they played a four ball match on Ormond Beach with the lowest better ball score declared the winner. Starting at Ormond and ending at The Clarendon at Seabreeze – a distance of four-and-a-half miles – it was considered the longest single 'hole' ever played.

## TALLY HO! CHOCKS AWAY

In the Second World War **Prince's Golf Club** on the south coast of England was taken over by the British Army as a practice firing range. Spitfire pilot P. B. 'Laddie' Lucas, whose father helped found the club many years before, found himself in a dogfight during the Battle of Britain in 1940. Running dangerously low on fuel and struggling to reach his base at Manston in Kent, he spotted Prince's clubhouse in the distance. Knowing the course like the back of his hand he selected one of the longer holes for an emergency landing. Overshooting the fairway, he and his aircraft crashed in the bushes somewhere behind the ninth green. A few days later, his friend and fellow golfer Henry Longhurst sent him a telegram that read: 'Bad driving. Poor show. I see you missed the fairway again…'

## KEEPING YOUR COOL WHEN BUNKERED

The removal of stone from a bunker at Royal Sydney Golf Club at Kose Bay, Australia, had the effect of turning the bunker into deadly **quicksand!** Edward Bayly Macarthur was playing with Mr N. H. Pope in late July when he sliced his drive from the tenth tee into this aptly named 'trap'. Taking his stance he rapidly began to sink and, realising the danger, tried to scramble out but could make no headway. He called to his playing partner for help and Mr Pope and two caddies ran to his aid. They were unable to pull him out. Macarthur, who weighed more than 14 stone (196lb), gradually sank deeper into the sand and was by now literally up to his neck in trouble. Thankfully, two naval men who were playing nearby heard the calls for help and managed to haul him to safety. The greens chairman immediately declared the bunker 'ground-under-repair'.

## HURRAH FOR EZAR

A loud mouth Texan named Joe Ezar entertained the Scottish gallery royally during the qualifying rounds for the British Open at Muirfield in 1935. A **quirky** character with a quick-fire putting method, he tossed his hat in the air after a good shot and began wisecracking loudly to his caddy. Barely glancing at the line before striking his putts, he shot two respectable rounds of 73 and 75 to make it into the tournament proper.

## NOT A BUDGET BREAK IN BENIDORM

The **Round-the-World Golf Club** began its second annual tour on 2 December 1926. Leaving New York aboard the *Empress of Scotland*, this twenty-strong group of enthusiastic and rich American golfers joined the Canadian Pacific world cruise. Quite an undertaking in the pre-air travel era, they would play golf in twenty countries over 132 days. They played courses in Egypt, India, China, Japan, the Philippines, Hawaii and Panama. In India the group was welcomed by Commander Collins, Secretary of the Royal Bombay Golf Club. The course was situated in a public park where the military performed its daily drill. While the putting greens were permanent, the 'bunkers' were temporary affairs made of canvas and attached to posts in

the ground. The sand was then emptied each afternoon to clear the field for cricket!

## SNAKES ALIVE?

George **Ribal** contended that a fear of snakes was the reason he had not paid his membership fees to the San Fernando Valley Golf Club in California. Sued for the debt, he was brought before Los Angeles Municipal Court in November 1931 where he told the judge: 'The first time I played that course I sliced into the rough. The caddy told me not to go after the ball because of rattlesnakes but I started in anyway. I killed one snake with a niblick before I was anywhere near the ball and I never did recover it. I went right back to the club-house and went home, and I've never been back.' Throwing some doubt on his story, V. N. Jaceard, representing the golf club, intimated that Ribal had been 'seeing snakes' where none existed.

## BRINGING GOLF TO THE MASSES

The **richest tournament in golf** took place at the Tam O' Shanter Country Club in Niles, Illinois, in 1942. The Tam O' Shanter Open (later called the All-American Open) was the brainchild of entrepreneur George Storr May and was the most innovative tournament of its era, ushering in many features that are now commonplace. He put up $15,000 as first prize – the largest purse in professional golf at the time. Where the USGA had charged $3.30 a ticket at the U.S. Open, he would only charge $1. He provided grandstands at key locations with large scoreboards so that fans could follow events happening elsewhere on the course. He even instigated shortwave radio so the scores could be updated minute-by-minute for the first time. He sold hot dogs, soda and beer at concession stands like those seen at baseball matches. He instigated a post-tournament charity dance, adorning the walls with slot machines. Won by Byron Nelson, the tournament was a huge success with around 40,000 spectators attending, with 23,000 on the final day alone. It did however have its critics: compared with the reverential hush of most tournaments, the Tam O'Shanter Open had a rowdy, boisterous atmosphere which many golf traditionalists objected to strongly. May did not help by arranging to have one player in his tournament compete wearing a mask and billing him as 'The Masked Marvel' or by paying a Scottish golfer to play wearing a kilt! He was also criticised after making a playing exception for heavyweight boxing champion Joe Louis. The *Saturday Evening Post* even wrote: 'All told, it was a cross between a county fair and a good airplane crash.'

## BULLETS, BOMBS AND BIRDIES

Wartime rules issued for **Richmond Golf Club** near London in 1941:

i. *A ball moved, lost or destroyed by enemy action may be replaced without penalty as near as possible to where it originally lay.*

ii. *During gunfire or enemy action, players may take shelter without penalty for ceasing play.*

iii. *The positions of known delayed action bombs are marked* by red and white flags and are placed at reasonably, but not guaranteed safe distances.

iv. A ball lying in a bomb crater may be lifted and dropped without penalty.

v. Players are asked to collect bomb and shell splinters from fairways to save damage to mowers. They may also be removed from the greens as loose impediments.

vi. If the ball enters a designated minefield, a new ball may be dropped without penalty within two-club lengths, not nearer the hole, without penalty.

## SCHOOL FOR BAGMEN

**Recommendations** for the education and training of caddies were published in 1912 by Mr Heinmann of the Agenda Club under the title *The Rough and the Fairway*. 163 pages long with a foreword by 'A.A.M.' the recommendations included (1) The elimination of all female caddies, saying that private golf clubs should only employ men or boys; (2) If boys are employed, there is a duty on the club to train them for alternative employment such as agriculture or carpentry; (3) Keep caddies informed of job vacancies in the Navy or Army; (4) Pay a fixed weekly wage with tips being extra; (5) Local schoolmasters should be advised of the boys' caddying activities.

## KEEP THE RED FLAG FLYING

The **Russian** Government announced in November 1933 that the first ever golf course would be opened in Moscow. Open for play the following spring, flags marking the holes would be in 'Communist Party' red. Caddies would be dressed in grey as befitting the typical Russian worker and instead of crying 'Fore!' local golfers would shout '*Davai*!' which is Russian for 'Give way!'

## SOUTH AFRICAN SCANDAL

Caddie Alfred **'Rabbit' Dyer** travelled to South Africa in 1974 with black professional Lee Elder as the guest of Brian Henning. Nicknamed 'Big Rabbit' for his ability to jump high at basketball, he was one of the first African American caddies to ply his trade on the PGA Tour, his most famous 'bag' being Gary Player with whom he had won the British Open at Royal Lytham earlier that year. Born into poverty, he was equally noted for his two-fisted solution to any hint of racist behaviour he encountered. One famous example happened during a pro-am in Swaziland when he laid out South African pro 'Big' Ben Baker. 'I was caddying for an American amateur in the pro-am,' said Rabbit, 'when he grabbed me and called me a kaffir... So I slugged him and knocked him out.' It was a similar story in England in the early 1980s when he ran into three local caddies while out taking yardages for Gary Player. It was getting late and they began harassing him, telling him to 'go home' and even stabbing him in the back with the grip end of a club! 'I didn't say much, I just hit the biggest one and knocked him out,' said Rabbit. The next day the paper headline read, 'Sugar Ray Rabbit!'

## PROFANITY PERMITTED

In **Rex versus Haddock** the defendant was charged under the Profane Oaths Act after cursing on a Cornish golf course in 1928. The standard penalty was a fine of 1 shilling per swearword for any manual labourer, soldier or seaman; 2 shillings for every other person under the degree of gentleman and 5 shillings for every person of or above the degree of gentleman. Mr Haddock was assessed as a gentleman and as he was heard to have cursed over 400 times, the court prosecutor demanded a fine of 100 pounds at a rate at of 5 shillings per curse! While pleading guilty the defendant contended that the fine was wrongly calculated: 'Golf by its very nature,' he contended, 'breaks down the normal restraints of a civilised citizen and so powerfully inflamed passions that it would be unjust to apply to my conduct the ordinary standards of law!' The presiding judge agreed and he was allowed to leave the court 'without a stain on his character'.

## HELD TO RANSOM

At a tournament in Texas in 1948 American pro Henry **Ransom** was alleged to have cheated by returning a wrongly marked scorecard. Officials wanted to hush it up but his playing partner Norman Von Nida was not going to let it pass. After a heated argument, the 6ft 2in Ransom punched the 5ft 6in Australian in the mouth: 'As I stumbled back I managed to grab him by the throat and closed my fingers on his windpipe,' Von Nida said later. 'My fingers were still like steel bars after my time at the meat works and Ransom was turning blue before the police arrived to break it up.'

## BUZZING THE OPEN

**Royal Air Force** flying instructor Marc Rodriguez's decision to swoop over a crowded course in Scotland landed him in front of a court martial on 15 April

2007. Flying just 400 feet above the ground he pleaded guilty to a charge of low flying during the Championship at Carnoustie. On 20 July, Rodriguez had turned to the student he was teaching and said:'Let's go and have a look at the golf.' An experienced pilot, he flew low over the tenth and the eighteenth holes before regaining height and flying back towards the North Sea, unaware that a spy satellite was tracking his flight and recording every movement. He had taken off from RAF Leuchars near St Andrews. Prosecuting counsel Squadron Leader Jim Morris told the hearing:'He even dipped the right wing of the aircraft so he could have a better view.' He was fined £1,500 and given a severe reprimand.

## BATTLE OF THE SEXES

A **revealing** survey was undertaken by *Golf for Women* and *Golf Digest* magazines in America in 2005 about male and female attitudes to golf. Nearly a quarter of those surveyed said there was no situation under which they would prefer to play with a member of the opposite sex! Only 14 per cent of men preferred to play with their spouse than with their male golfing buddies. But the most interesting stat of all was revealed by the question: 'Would you be willing to give up sex for a year for a round at Augusta?' The survey showed that 31% of men and 32% of women would.

## HOT STUFF

A major grass fire began in **Reno**, Nevada, in June 2007 after a golfer hit a rock in the rough that created a spark. Turning twenty acres of tinder dry brush into an inferno, it took fifty firefighters to bring it under control as it threatened to engulf nearby homes.

## A SPANISH SHORTFALL

**Rafael Cabrera-Bello** was disqualified after eleven holes of the second round of the South African Open on 18 December 2010 having lost all eleven balls in his bag! The highly rated Spanish professional was 11 over par for his first ten holes and although Rule 4-4a allows a golfer to borrow extra equipment with the exception of clubs from a playing partner or an outside agency, almost all pro tournaments are played under the 'one ball' rule, meaning

that only one type of ball can be played in each round. Therefore he had no choice but to disqualify himself and walk in.

## GOLF IS A DANGEROUS GAME

'**Survival** tips for the over 50s!' was published in January 1925 by *Golf Illustrated* magazine under the heading: 'HEALTH RULES FOR VETERAN GOLFERS'. They included:

1. *All golfers over fifty should have a thorough physical inventory taken of themselves at least once a year.*
2. *Golfers over fifty who have heart, kidney or blood pressure trouble should play the game in a way consistent with their physical limitations.*
3. *They should not play at all if the game induces marked shortness of breath, vertigo, pain about the heart or palpitations;*
4. *Golfers with cardio-vascular handicaps should avoid – Playing on a very hilly or crowded course; Playing more than eighteen*

holes daily; Playing directly after eating; Playing competitively; Playing on very hot, very cold, or very windy days; Playing when physically tired or indisposed; Playing very irregularly; Playing vigorously, i.e., pressing or over swinging; Playing with their wives; Playing with experts or much younger golfers.

5. All golfers over fifty should take a hot shower—not a cold one—on completion of the game.

6. All golfers over fifty should take, provided it is qualitatively and quantitatively controlled —one highball on the nineteenth hole with 2 oz of Scotch. Cocktails are strictly tabooed.

## DOUBLE SHOCK

**Sotheby's auction house** offered a free golf memorabilia valuation service at their offices in Edinburgh in 1992. Halfway through the day a local man popped in with a handful of wooden shafted clubs in a tatty canvas bag. Imagine his surprise when one of them turned out to be an extremely rare blacksmith-made iron from the early 1700s initially valued around £30,000. Then picture how he felt when it eventually sold to Jamie Ortiz-Patino, billionaire owner of Valderrama Golf Club in Spain, for a record sum of £92,400! Speaking afterward, the original owner described how he had kept the club in his garden shed for years and it was only brought out when his grandchildren wanted something to dig the garden up with!

## WATER PROBLEMS

Two men were charged with assault at **Springfield Golf Course** in South Union, Pennsylvania, in August 2014. According to police, a sixty-three-year-old man struck a forty-two-year-old man with a golf club after an argument started on the fifth hole of the Springdale Golf Course over the rule regarding casual water. With the course spotted with pools of water after a recent downpour, the younger man said he didn't know the rule and deferred to a senior golfer of their five-member group. A heated debate ensued, which began again on the following hole – this time over placement of the ball on the fairway. 'You didn't know the rule on five, and suddenly you're an expert when it benefits you,' said one man who questioned the lift and place. 'That was the gist of why it ignited and why it got heated up.' Trooper Mrosko reported that the forty-two-year-old was struck on the head and arm with a golf club and the older man suffered a broken lip and swelling on his face. Describing both injuries as minor, the Trooper explained the blow was less forceful than it could have been because the man gripped the club near its head with one hand. Both were treated and released from Uniontown Hospital a short time later.

## BIRDS EYE VIEW GOLF

An unusual match took place at **Sonning Golf Club** near Reading in April 1930 between a former RAF pilot and the club professional, A. J. Young. Captain G. A. B. Pennington flew over the course and was deemed to have 'holed out' whenever he dropped the ball on a green. If he missed, then he was deemed to have taken two strokes 'from the edge' and not surprisingly went round in just 29 'strokes!' Having scored 69, Young immediately called for a return match in which Captain Pennington, after dropping his ball on each green, would land on a nearby fairway and putt out in the orthodox manner! The result of the second match is unknown but a local newspaper noted the 'foolhardy' nature of the challenge.

## SLUMMING IT

**Sun Microsystems** co-founder Scott McNealy officially became the richest caddie in history after looping for his son Maverick McNealy at the 2014 U.S. Open sectional qualifying in Daly City, California. With an estimated personal wealth rated around the 1 billion dollars mark, he expressed his desire to continue carrying for his son, a freshman at Stanford, after Maverick finished third and qualified for the Championship proper at Pinehurst.

## THE COAL MINERS GOLF CLUB

The owners of the **Seghill Colliery** in Northumberland in northern England opened a nine-hole golf course for miners and their families in 1929. One of the most progressive coal mines in the United Kingdom, the subscription was set at six pennies a week and was available to any of the 1,000-plus workers. By the time in opened in June the club already had 150 members. A local professional was then employed to coach any novices thinking of taking up the game. The only rule was that players had to wear collars and ties and be fully shaved when playing golf.

## FALSE ALARM

H. Richard **Stamer** of Asbury Park, New Jersey was playing a four-ball match at the Colonial Terrace public course in 1930. Hooking his approach to the ninth he heard a crashing sound but could not find his ball. Minutes later he spotted a fire truck pulling up to the clubhouse, lights and sirens blazing. His hooked brassie shot had struck a fire alarm on the side of the clubhouse, broken the glass and set off the bell. As the alarm was linked to the local fire house they immediately dispatched a fire truck to deal with the emergency!

## ROCKET SCIENCE

Scientist **Maximilian Richard Speiser** invented the first computerised golf simulator in 1963. Developed from a system he had invented for tracking low-flying ballistic missiles, it was called Golf-O-Tron. Not unlike simulators used today, the player aimed at an illuminated picture of a fairway 17 feet away. The elapsed time between the sound of club on ball and the ball's impact on screen enabled the computer to calculate the length of drive and probable roll within five yards. Golfers had a choice of playing five courses costing $1.50 to $5 depending on the number of holes played.

## STYMIED!

Professor Frank **Stewart Smith** courted controversy in 1931 when he said that there was no such thing as a **stymie**! No longer in use, this was the name given to a situation when the golfers putting line was blocked by an opponent's ball. Unthinkable today, the 'stymie' included any putt from lengthy lay-ups to a two-inch tap-in! In common use across the globe, Smith maintained that if a player had sufficient skill and knew how to apply it, any stymie could be overcome. Raising much debate, Smith, an amateur golfer, was called upon to prove his statement that: '9 out of 10 stymies were quite easy to play.' So much so that a test was arranged with all his critics present, plus a battery of motion-picture cameras ready to record the action. Professor Smith then

confounded everyone by negotiating the most difficult of stymies three times out of four – even the hardest one where two balls were touching just inches away from the cup... This, of course, completely undermined the case of anyone who wanted the stymie abolished at the time.

## SPACEMAN SULLY

Andy **Sullivan**, a European Tour professional from Nuneaton in England, won the most unusual hole-in-one prize ever offered in professional golf – a trip to outer space! 'Sully' made his 'space ace' at the par 3, fifteenth hole at Kennemer Golf & Country Club during the final round of the KLM (Dutch) Open on 14 September 2014. Winning a seat on a future space excursion from sponsor XCOR Space Expeditions, his out-of-this-world excursion will be available in the second half of 2015. With the trip valued at $95,000, the space craft will take off from a launch pad in the Mojave Desert and will travel almost 39 miles into space before coming back to Earth. Sullivan, who required medical treatment for altitude sickness while competing in the European Masters in the Swiss Alps a few weeks later, hedged his bets when discussing whether or not he would accept the prize. 'I will have to speak to the wife first,' he said sheepishly.

## CITY SLICKERS

Richard **Sutton** bet fellow stockbroker Toby Milbanke that he could hit a golf ball from the south side of Tower Bridge in the City of London to the top of St James's Street in less than 2,000 strokes. Attempting the feat on Sunday, 26 April 1939, he used nothing but his putter and completed the 'course' in 142 to win his wager easily. Milbanke who accepted the over-generous figure of 2,000 strokes felt confident the police would stop his opponent long before he got to his destination! Sutton was indeed stopped four or five times but his antagonist hadn't reckoned on the sporting instincts of the London bobbies. To the disappointment of Milbanke, each time they threatened to arrest his opponent he explained that he was 'doing it for a bet' and they let him proceed! Speaking to reporters afterwards, Sutton said that he played the full round with the same ball, hitting no pedestrians or vehicles and doing no damage. He also employed a street urchin to caddy for him who: 'proudly, if grubbily, filled in my scorecard and was extremely useful looking for the ball, watching out for traffic and similar tasks.'

## STEAK WARS!

In the lead-up to the 1949 Ryder Cup at Ganton Golf Club, huge controversy ensued between the visiting U.S. team captained by Ben Hogan and their British hosts. Known as 'Steak Wars', it revolved around the decision to bring along 600 beef steaks, plus dozens of sides of bacon and hams, for their trip to the United Kingdom. They arrived at Southampton on board the *Queen Elizabeth* on 11 September, when customs officials must have choked at the sight of this best rump steak as it entered the country in refrigerated units. With rationing still in place, every time the American team picked up a newspaper all they read about was their luxurious eating habits! Hogan explained that it was to be shared with their hard-up opponents at various functions but the British PGA was having none of it. Hogan was incensed: 'Do people think we are going to eat all those steaks ourselves?' he said. A few days later Hogan demanded a look at the British team's irons the evening before the match was due to begin. He suggested they were illegally grooved and the argument (which threatened the entire match) was settled only minutes before the first match teed off. Hogan had his revenge, the Americans retained the cup, but the gentlemanly reputation of the competition was dented for ever.

## SPARKY WINS THE BIG ONE

Frank **Stranahan** won the British Amateur Championship at St Andrews in May 1948. Heir to the Toledo, Ohio, Champion Spark Plugs fortune, he is one of the game's strangest and most fascinating characters. Touring the world playing golf, when he was not getting expensive advice from golf pros he spent countless hours in his private gym building up his muscles by lifting 150lb dumb bells. Number one power lifter in his weight class from 1945 to

1954, he became known as the 'Toledo Strongman'. Frank's stated ambition in life was to win the U.S. Amateur Golf Championship, which he came close to on a number of occasions. After losing to Arnold Palmer in the 1954 U.S. Amateur Championship he made the decision to turn professional at the late age of thirty-two. Winner of seventy events, he never recaptured that amateur form but still won a creditable four events and finished second to Ben Hogan in the 1953 British Open.

## HEAD CASE

Pennsylvania **State Police** investigated a strange case involving 'decapitated' golf clubs in the Pittsburgh area in 2011. Surveillance pictures showed a well-dressed couple removing heads from thirteen expensive drivers worth about $300 to $400 each in five different incidents between 14 and 21 February at Dick's Sporting Goods stores in Greensburg, West Mifflin, Robinson Township and South Hills. Investigators believe the couple were re-using the stolen driver heads to make custom clubs – or selling the stolen heads onto a third party. The clubs were all priced for retail but the security code was on the shafts so the couple could leave with the stolen heads without triggering anti-theft alarms. No immediate arrests were expected, said the police.

## THAWED OUT

Harry **Thaw** hit the headlines in January 1908 after sending in his membership subscription to Pittsburgh Golf Club from his prison cell in the State Penitentiary. The covering letter had just one word – 'Bunkered!'

## TITANIC SWITCHEROO

Alvin Clarence Thomas died in 1974. Better known as the notorious gambler and golf hustler **'Titanic' Thompson**, he reputedly won huge sums gambling at golf in the 1930s. His favourite con was to win thousands of dollars playing right-handed before switching to left-handed clubs to give his victims a chance to win their money back. Imagine their reaction when he played even better! What none of them knew was he was naturally left-handed and played better that way.

## PERFECT REPLY

In the run-up to the 1954 **United States Open** at Baltusrol, course designer Robert Trent-Jones added a water hazard to the front of the 185-yard par 3 fourth on the Lower Course, thereby upsetting a small but vocal group of Baltusrol members. The legendary course designer's patience finally ran out. Challenging the idea that it was now almost impossible to carry the lake from the back tee, RTJ volunteered to play the hole himself. With barely a practice swing he took out a 4 iron and slammed it straight into the hole for an ace! 'Gentlemen,' said Trent-Jones, 'that should settle all arguments.'

## WAR ON THE SHORE

The **USA** won the 1991 Ryder Cup in controversial circumstances. Played on the Ocean Course at Kiawah Island Golf Resort in South Carolina, tension between the two teams was at an all-time high. In a dramatic conclusion that saw Bernhard Langer miss a six-foot par putt for victory which would have clinched a 14-all tie and retain the Ryder Cup for Europe, the home team won by 14½ to 13½ points. A bad tempered affair throughout, the bad blood which had been festering since the 1989 competition between Seve Ballesteros and Paul Azinger erupted once more with Azinger saying, 'I can tell you we're not trying to cheat' and Ballesteros retorting, 'Oh no. Breaking the rules and cheating are two different things.' The Americans Azinger and Chip Beck had switched the ball, probably more than once, in the Friday foursomes, in violation of the one-ball rule. No wonder it was named the 'War on the Shore.'

## ROCK 'N' ROLLIN AT THE RYDER CUP

Calling it the **'ultimate'** item of Ryder Cup memorabilia is stretching it a touch, but the police car which sped Rory McIlroy through the Chicago suburbs in time to make his Ryder Cup singles *tee time* was offered for sale in an online auction website. Now part of golfing folklore, a mix-up over his Sunday morning *tee time* in 2012 left the world No.1 facing instant disqualification and his team almost certain defeat. Step forward Pat Rollins, deputy chief of police of Lombard where the European team were based. Driving an unmarked Ford Crown Victoria, he radioed local traffic cops to clear each intersection en route to the Medinah Country Club. He got him there just in time to take a couple of practice swings. Rory beat Keegan Bradley and Europe eventually retained the trophy by one point. Built in 2005 and with 81,000 miles on the clock, it can hardly be classed as 'one careful owner'. Yet it did play its part in Ryder Cup history and at the time of going to print, was expected to sell for at least ten-times its $3,000 book price! 'Some of my colleagues have jokingly said the United States might have won the Ryder Cup if it wasn't for that old Ford,' said Officer Rollins.

## FATAL WAGER

In one of the most **unusual golfing bets** ever recorded, Sir David Moncrieff of Moncrieff, Bart 'backed his life against the life of John Whyte-Melville, Esq. of Strathkiness' in a match that took place on 3 November 1820. While the exact terms of the bet were unknown, they both agreed that the 'survivor' should present the Society of St Andrews Golfers with a silver putter.

## DRESSING DOWN

*Vogue* magazine in the United States was highly critically of British female golfers in 1928: 'In Britain, most lady golfers continue to appear in crumpled pullovers, shapeless skirts and deplorable hats and skirts. Another fashion commentator suggested that female clothing came in just three styles – 'dull, dark and drab'. This was not helped by the LGU who introduced guidelines which insisted on stocking-covered legs, a ban on colourful clothing, pleated skirts and rolling up of sleeves during the summer months.

## FORE!

**Valentine William Neville Green**, fourteen, was killed in a tragic accident at Tuai in New Zealand in May 1929.

Evidence provided at the Coroners Court showed that he was struck on the carotid artery on the left side of the neck by a woman practising with her new clubs. The first Mrs McGarry knew of the accident was when Green exclaimed, 'You've knocked me out.' He walked a couple of paces, gasped, and sank to the ground, dying immediately. A verdict of accidental death was returned with no blame attached to any third party.

## NEVER TALK TO STRANGERS, OR PLAY GOLF WITH THEM

Visitors to **Van Cortlandt Park Public Golf Course** in 1912 in the Bronx area of New York City became used to seeing a golfer wearing a black mask, black clothes, and black plush cap playing on the course. Despite inquiries, nothing was learned of the identity of the stranger except that he spoke with an English accent and styled himself 'the Black Masker'. Hitting the ball miles off the tee, he was known to have played for large amounts of money. In November the mystery deepened when he issued an open challenge to U.S. Open champion John J. McDermott. He would play three matches of thirty-six holes each on level terms for a stake of not less than $1,000. The match would be scheduled for any first-class course in the Metropolitan area and on any date suitable to him. Not surprisingly, McDermott turned down the offer.

## UNTRAINED CADDIES

**Van Cortlandt Park Public Golf Course story two**; a new City regulation in 1899 forced the caddies who worked at the course in the Bronx area of New York to wear identification badges, hoping to stem a rising tide of crime. Most of the caddies came from the lower classes who knew and cared little about golf etiquette. What they were expert in was pick-pocketing. Golfers who took the train up to Van Cortlandt Park often complained about the: 'small army of yelling, howling caddies' who travelled with them in the morning. *The New York Times* reported how: 'Urchins roam unrestricted, intent upon fleecing every strange golfer out of as much money as can be extorted, while cases have often occurred where balls were purposely not found that had been driven into high grass or into a woody section. An unemployed confederate keeps his eye on the spot, however, and when the player has passed from sight the ball is picked up, and perhaps sold for a dime to the very man who lost it.'

169

## PARTING COMPANY

**Walter Hagen** was divorced by his second wife Edna Strauss in late 1927. Describing her life with the golfing legend she said: 'Unless a woman is a golf addict herself, she should never marry a confirmed golfer. It can only go on the rocks. Walter lived golf, asleep and awake. Before dinner and after he was practicing strokes in the living room…'

## HAVE YOU EVER SEEN ANYTHING LIKE THAT?

Tiger **Woods** won the Masters at Augusta National on 10 April 2005. In a dramatic final round of a rain-disrupted event, he hit one of the most memorable shots in the history of the game. Aiming at right-angles to the hole on the par 3 sixteenth he used the massive slopes that run through the back of this green to chip in for a birdie. A virtually impossible shot, his ball fell into the hole after looking like it was going to hang on the edge. Forever known as the 'Nike ball' shot after the brand of ball he used, Verne Lundquist of CBS uttered the immortal words: 'Oh my goodness! Oh wow! In your life have you ever seen anything like that?' Giving him a two-shot advantage, two bogeys on the last two holes saw him finish level with fellow American Chris DiMarco on 276. The first play-off in Masters History to start at the eighteenth, Tiger made a superb birdie-3 to win. Accepting the green jacket, a tearful Woods dedicated his victory to his gravely ill father who was watching at home in California.

## SEXIST GOLF HEADWEAR?

A golf hat made of solid **wood** went on sale in London in 1928. Made especially for women golfers it was aimed at protecting them from the danger of flying balls hit by men! Imaginatively named the 'Woodenhead', it was priced at a not inconsiderable £10.

## WEIGHED DOWN

English opera singer Harry Dearth created a sensation by playing a round of golf clad in a full suit of armour. The result of a **wager**, the only condition was that he appeared on the links in the heavy suit of chain mail that he wore in his role of St George in Sir Edward Elgar's The Crown of India. Played before a large gallery, the armour proved too great a handicap, for after a close struggle Mr Dearth was beaten two up and one to play.

## UPWARDLY MOBILE

Noted English golf course architect, Charles Alison was playing in a match at **Woking Golf Club** near London in 1931 when his approach to the final green landed on the clubhouse roof! Borrowing a ladder, he climbed up in front of a large crowd below before calmly chipping the ball back onto the green. Moments later he holed his putt and halved the game.

## BY ROYAL COMMAND

HRH Edward, Prince of **Wales** was widely known as the 'keenest golfer in the Kingdom'. His personal professional was Archibald Compston of Coombe Hill Golf Club in

Surrey. A no-nonsense character, even Archie was astonished when he received an urgent telegram from chic Biarritz in September 1932. He was in Ireland at the time and the Prince, frustrated by his poor golf, had ordered him over to France to give him a lesson! Next day Archie left Ireland for Biarritz to coach his royal pupil back to form.

## SECRET NIGHT-TIME GOLFER

Police from the **Werribee district** of Melbourne in Australia admitted they were baffled by an unusual incident which took place on 28 February 2010. A woman was struck on the head by a golf ball that flew in through her taxi window while she was being driven home. Adding to the confusion it was late at night and the local golf course was shut! Struck hard enough that it fractured her skull, the unfortunate woman spent nearly two weeks in hospital. Thankfully she made a full recovery but the phantom night-time golfer remains at large.

## BRITISH PLUCK

Captain George Morris of the British Army bet he could complete ten rounds of golf on the **Walmer and Kingsdown** golf course in Deal within 24 hours and in fewer than 900 strokes. He began at 4 a.m. on 10 August 1934, when visibility was limited to just 50 yards. After three rounds he stopped for a short break and enjoyed three eggs in milk and brandy for breakfast. Two rounds later he enjoyed a lunch of lettuce and ginger beer! He changed his golf ball for the first time after five rounds. It was only after completing the sixth round that he changed his shoes. After the eighth round signs of weariness became apparent. He finally completed his tenth and last round after 17 hours 20 minutes. He took 889 strokes with the lowest round being 84 and the highest (and last) of 97. The massive sum of £3,000 in side bets was known to have changed hands during the day. Not long afterward, invalided war hero Captain R. Norman won a wager of his own after completing ten non-stop rounds at Stoke Poges Golf Club in June. Betting that he could shoot under 1,000 strokes he took 960. His best-round was 89 and worst 107 against a par of 75. He took 16 hours and 30 minutes and walked an estimated 45 miles.

## WHO NEEDS GOLF?

A **'World No-Golf Day'** was organised by the grandly titled: 'Global Network for Anti-Golf Course Action'. Scheduled for April 1993 it followed a three-day conference on 'Golf Course and Resort Development in the Asia-Pacific Region in Panang, Malaysia.' Complaining that golf courses are bad for the environment, they demanded an 'immediate moratorium on all golf course development; an open and public environmental and social review/audit of existing golf courses and that all existing golf courses should be converted to public parks, and where they lie in forest areas, wetlands and islands, there should be rehabilitation and regeneration of the land to its natural state.' Not surprisingly, the golf course developers politely ignored their proposal.

GOLF. " ONE UP — TWO TO PLAY."

## TALK ABOUT RECYCLING

**W.J. Robinson**, professional at St Margaret's at Cliffe Golf Club in Kent, sliced his drive on the eighteenth hole in June 1934. Hitting a cow in a nearby field on the back of the head, the ball killed the unfortunate animal outright. Compensating the local farmer for the loss, the members had the animal chopped into cuts of succulent meat by a local butcher and had the horns mounted for a new competition called the Cow's Horn Cup!

## SWING FOR IT

Inveterate thief **Truman Wiltshire** was found guilty of stealing a set of golf clubs and lawnmower from an unnamed golf club in the south of England in 1935. Asked by the arresting officer Inspector Jeffries why he had so much golf equipment in his home, he said that he had simply 'borrowed them from a pal' because he intended to play golf. Taken outside he was asked to grip the club and swing it but according to Jeffries, 'demonstrated no aptitude for the game whatsoever.' Not surprisingly, he was jailed for nine months with an order given to return the stolen equipment.

## EXPENSIVE DRINK!

The United States PGA Championship medal won by **Walter Hagen** in 1925 sold at auction for approximately $62,000 in November 2011. Engraved 'Professional Golfers Association of America', the 2-inch diameter gold medal with a set diamond in the front was engraved with Hagen's name on the reverse side. According to the auction catalogue it was reputedly left as collateral for a bar bill in Palm Springs, California and never reclaimed!

## LET SLIP THE DOGS OF WAR

England declared **war** against Germany at 11.00 a.m. on Sunday, 3 September 1939. Not long before, a group of golfers teed-off at Royal St George's Golf Club in Sandwich, Kent. They included long-time member Douglas Grant, who asked the steward to raise the clubhouse flag if war was declared. Up by the time they reached the turn, the golfers decided to continue to the back-nine, war or no. Then an air raid siren suddenly blasted out causing Grant to shank the ball into a bunker. Red-faced with anger he ordered his caddie to pick up the ball, famously saying: 'If this damn war is going to spoil my golf, I will pop over to Germany and have a word with Herr Hitler myself!'

## BAD EDITING

Filming began on Shell's *Wonderful World of Golf* at Pine Valley in New Jersey. The first match was between Byron Nelson and Gene Littler in 1961 but it was not the first match that aired the following year. Using cameramen totally unfamiliar with the game, nobody told them to keep their cameras focused on the ball until it stopped rolling. So when the time came to edit the film all they had was the ball in flight! The only solution was to go back to New Jersey some months later and shoot additional footage using little-known professional, Leo Fraser, to hit the shots. On the actual show, after Nelson hit his opening drive a cameraman got off his truck, grabbed the ball and threw it back toward the tee. 'Ask him to hit it again,' he shouted over the radio, 'we missed it!'

## WACKY WYKAGYL WAR GAMES

**Wykagyl Country Club** in New Rochelle, New York, agreed to stage war games on its fairways in June 1942. As war raged in Europe, the Club gave permission to the 105th Regiment of the Second Field Artillery of the New York Guard to hold a one day practice battle on the links. But it was the announcement that the battle would take place on a Sunday that brought a storm of controversy. Berated by local church groups, the matter was debated back and forth for days in the New York newspapers, Sabbath or otherwise, Club officials argued that it was 'unpatriotic' not to go ahead. On the day, several hundred soldiers were divided into two armies named the Reds and the Blues. The Reds'

task was to defend the knoll near the ninth and twelfth tees. The Blues' commander was Colonel Arthur Farrell who set up camp at the third green and began his advance from there. According to one report, members of the Blue Army foolishly tried to ford the stream that divides the fifth and sixth fairways. Showing a complete lack of local knowledge, many became stuck in the quicksand bottom and sank to their hips in the clawing mud. Dr Joe Refsum, an umpire for the battle, was forced to pull two or three out of the stream in case fake fatalities became real ones. The battle went on for most of the day. The defending Red Army under the command of Lieutenant Colonel Peter Forsman,

Wykagyl's Club Champion in both 1939 and 1940, beat off attack after attack. The turning point came when a smoke screen laid down by the Blues was blown away by a gust of wind, revealing the attacking army. They were suddenly bombarded by blank fire and beaten back. They also faced a barrage of rock-hard crab apples thrown by a group of enthusiastic Wykagyl junior members who had been seconded into the Reds. *The New Rochelle Standard Star* newspaper reported the important part they played in the victory: 'the manoeuvres had been a success, casualties had been excessive and the youngsters were effective.'

## FACEBOOK FRENZY

A **Wisconsin** golf course owner who advertised nine holes of golf for $9.11 in 2013 to mark the 12th anniversary of the September 11 terrorist attacks, received death threats after his offer became public via the Internet. The discount, which also included eighteen holes of golf at Tumbledown Trails Golf Course near Madison for $19.11, was only good for the day but after a backlash on Facebook, owner and general manager Marc Watts considered actually closing the course. Having received a threat to burn down the clubhouse at the family-operated public golf course, the local sheriff's department sent a deputy to guard the property. 'We're a little hurt by the fact that people are putting such a negative context on this,' said Watts. 'I thought people would appreciate it.'

## GOBBY AND SNOBBY

**Walter J. Travis** (see photo, page 182) became the first non-British winner of the 1904 Amateur Championship at Royal St George's Golf Club in Sandwich, Kent. (Originally from Australia he had taken American citizenship a few years earlier.) Regarded as aloof because he refused social engagements to concentrate on his golf, Travis began the week by complaining about being assigned a caddie he later described as, 'a natural-born idiot and cross-eyed at that'. Refused a change of bagman, he determinedly beat top British players Harold Hilton and Horace Hutchinson on the way to the final, where he defeated the long-hitting Edward Blackwell by 4 & 3. At the prize-giving Lord Northbourne reflected the feelings of many when he said: 'Never since the days of Caesar has the British nation been subjected to such humiliation.' Many observers felt the cigar-puffing Travis's use of a new-style centre-shafted mallet putter known as the 'Schenectady' was tantamount to cheating. *Golf Illustrated* magazine in England described his historic victory in dismissive terms: 'The American holed a putt of twenty yards on nearly every green, his driving was childlike in its shortness, and he was smoking himself to death at the time.' The first man to hold both titles after winning the 1903 U.S. Amateur Championship, Travis never played in the British Amateur again. As the reigning U.S. and British Amateur champ, *The New York Times* declared him the 'World Champion of Golf.'

## TIGER CUB

Following a news story that two-year old Tiger **Woods** had shot 48 for nine-holes over the Navy Golf Course where his father Earl was a member, he was invited to appear on the Mike Douglas Television Show. Proving a hit with the studio audience, Tiger nervously putts against comic legend Bob Hope with movie star Jimmy Stewart looking on in amazement. Sadly, the publicity from his appearance annoyed some of the members at the NGC and they banned any golfer under the age of ten from using the course. As a consequence, Earl moved Tiger to a par 3 course in Long Beach, where he would later take lessons from local teaching professional, Rudy Duran. Age six, Tiger was able to reach the greens from the tees. He even made a couple of holes-in-one.

## EXTREME GOLF

The one-hole golf course at Camp Bonifas in Panmunjom, South Korea is labelled the **'World's Most Dangerous Golf Course'** in a *Sports Illustrated* article in 1988. Located barely 400 metres from the southern boundary of the

Demilitarised Zone (DMZ) which forms the border between South Korea and North Korea, Bonifas is home to the United Nations Command Security Battalion whose primary mission is to monitor and enforce the Armistice agreement of 1953. An area of extreme military tension, the hole has an Astroturf green and is surrounded on three sides by minefields. Popular with the troops who monitor the DMZ, there were reports that the course had seen at least one errant shot explode hidden land mines.

## GOLF BALLS FOR SALE AT A PRICE

*The Wall Street Journal* reported in July 2009 how 'war creates an economic logic of its own…' Highlighting the strange economy of war-torn Afghanistan, it noted how the U.S. military 'pays out as much as $25 million a month to Afghan Companies.' Listing some of the more bizarre deals that were struck, apart from major road building contracts they included buying blocks of ice, fragments of spent rockets and even used golf balls from locals. The balls were the same ones the military struck from their makeshift driving range situated on top of a latrine building. Local boys scrambled to collect any that carry a local river and came to rest in terraced fields beyond. They then sold them back to the soldiers for ten cents each.

## THE BLAME GAME

James **Walsh**, Sales Manager of the tank division of Bethlehem Steel in New Jersey was blinded in his left eye during a round of golf in 1964. Playing in a company day at the Manufacturers Golf and Country Club in Oreland, Pennsylvania, he sued his playing partner William Sellers and the heating business he owned for $250,000. Claiming that Sellers had negligently failed to wipe his hands before swinging, he alleged that this had caused him to mishit the ball in his direction. Lawyers acting for Sellers moved to have the suit dismissed on the grounds that anyone who plays golf automatically 'assumes the risk of being struck by a ball' and is thus barred from seeking damages. A few months later Judge Alfred Luongo of the Philadelphia U.S. District Court surprised the golfing world by ruling in Mr Walsh's favour. In his summing up, he agreed that while every golfer 'assumes the risk or is guilty of contributory negligence if he intentionally or carelessly walks ahead or stands within the orbit of the shot of a person playing behind him,' he felt that it did not apply to this particular case. It appeared that when the ball was struck, Walsh was sitting in a golf cart some 20 ft behind the tee. Considered a place of safety he therefore could not be said to have 'voluntarily assumed the risk' of not being injured. Worse still, he ordered the Defendant Sellers to stand trial.

## BORN LUCKY

British pensioner Peter **Wafford** beat odds of 67 million to 1 by scoring two aces in a single round of golf. Mr Wafford, 75, who has played golf for just six years, sunk the pair of aces during a veterans match at Chigwell Golf Club in Essex on 17 May 2010. He used a seven wood for both par 3 holes. 'Quite often the ball hits a rock or a tree and bounces back onto the green but they both went straight in,' he said. 'I didn't realise the significance at first, and I wasn't expecting so much attention, but I think it has cost me about 200 quid (£200) in drinks.'

## SNAKE EGGS

A collector paid $1,401 in 2008 for a collection of golf balls that had been surgically removed from a python! The lot included the **X-ray** of the balls inside the reptile shortly before surgery took place. Scattered around an Australian hen house in an effort to get the birds to lay more, the 15-foot long snake mistook them for real eggs but was unable to digest them. Taken to the Currumbin Wildlife Sanctuary on Australia's Gold Coast, the story attracted a degree of publicity when the vet who removed them put them into an online auction to raise money for a new wildlife hospital. After some intense bidding that went down to the last second, the balls were sold to an Australian man. As for Slippery Sid, the python made a full recovery and was released into the wild but a long way from any local golf course!

## RORY ROARING AWAY FROM HIS RIVALS

One modern day golfer gifted with the **X-factor** is Irishman Rory McIlroy. Since making his first ever appearance on the European Tour in the British Masters at the Forest of Arden Golf and Country Club in Warwickshire a few days after his sixteenth birthday on 4 May 2005, he has gone from strength to strength, major success to major success. Challenging Tiger Woods as the biggest name in golf, he turned professional on 19 September 2007, the day before competing in the Quinn Direct British Masters at the Belfry in Warwickshire. He finished in a tie for 42nd place. McIlroy then finished in third place at the Alfred Dunhill Links Championship in October. McIlroy became the youngest Affiliate Member in the history of The European Tour to earn a player's card. The next week, he secured his card for the 2008 season by finishing in a tie for fourth place at the Open de Madrid Valle Romano. He finished the season in 95th place on the Order of Merit with official earnings of €277,255. Since then he has captured four major championships as well as made numerous Ryder Cup appearances.

## SPEEDING UP GOLF

Chet W. **Young** copyrighted an unusual idea in December 1948 to speed up tournament play entitled 'The Theatre of Golf'. Outlining his idea in a letter to Fred Corcoran of the American PGA, he proposed that play would be conducted over just one hole with grandstands on either side. Played in both directions with a green at either end, each 'round' would be played from a series of tees measuring anywhere from 130 yards to a full par-five hole at 530 yards! Unlike normal pro tournaments, play could be scheduled, 'every hour of the day and night' with the help of massive floodlights. In a radical departure from the norm he suggested that 'paying customers move right along with the play using a rolling gallery grandstand!' He also proposed that after every tee shot, 'players ride on stands with the gallery (then) down the fairway to the next shot. The stands move at twice the walking speed or about ten miles an hour... A full eighteen-hole match should be played in about an hour and a quarter (with) each moving gallery stand seating 2,000 fans...' Convinced that golf would suffer unless four-hour rounds were eliminated he concluded: 'If such an idea could be installed in most of the larger cities of America it would be possible to schedule (professional) golf matches much like a vaudeville act is booked right now and we eliminate the bad element of the excessive time required to complete a match...'

## POWER GOLF SUMO STYLE

Japanese sumo wrestler **Yokozuna Tochinishiki** credited golf for strengthening his legs on the occasion of his 499th career victory in 1960. 'The only problem I have,' said the 29-stone legend, 'is seeing the ball when I tee it up.'

## YANCEY BOTTLED OUT

In the second round of the 1964 U.S. Open at the Blue Course of Congressional Country Club in Bethesda, Maryland, pro Bert **Yancey** hit his approach into a pond hard by the eighteenth green in the second round on 19 June. Knowing that a par would see him safe for the weekend, He took off his right shoe and sock and played his ball onto the edge of the green. He then realised that he had sliced his foot open on a broken bottle! He missed the putt and knowing that he had missed the cut he picked his ball up and headed straight to a local hospital for stitches.

## MARKED FOR LIFE

Two local **youths** pleaded not guilty at St Andrews Police Court in 1896 to deliberately moving the tee markers on the seventeenth hole at St Andrews for pecuniary advantage. Caught red-handed moving the blocks 25 yards nearer to the boundary wall from their position behind the sixteenth green, their plan was to force golfers to play over the corner of the wall – very much like today. On the morning in question, the accused had been seen hanging around in the Station Master's garden, having 'set a trap for the players'. Not unlike the shot facing golfers today, the idea was any stray drive would end up out-of-bounds in the Station Master's garden. Hidden by the large wooden sheds which blocked the view, they would gather up any 'lost' balls before selling them on to other unsuspecting golfers later the same day! Passing a guilty verdict, Judge Barr said it was, 'diabolical to interfere with the natural course of sport in this way' and imposed the full penalty of £1 on the two miscreants.

## GOLF BY ANY OTHER NAME WOULD PLAY AS WET

China staged the world's first underwater golf tournament at **Zuohai Aquarium** in Fuzhou City. It involved five players in a 50ft-deep tank. 'Whoever gets the ball in the hole first wins the match,' an aquarium spokesman told the People's Daily newspaper: 'The only difference is that players are judged on how long it took them to complete the hole rather than the number of strokes taken…' Fish and mammals distract the players, and their buoyancy makes it hard for them to stabilise themselves. Water currents also make the trajectory of the ball hard to predict. The winner sank the ball in just one minute and twenty seconds, while the one who came last took five minutes.

## MURDER ON THE LINKS

On 10 February 2010 an Indonesian court found the country's former anti-corruption czar guilty of murdering prominent business executive, Nasrudin **Zulkarnaen**. Antasari Azhar, fifty-six, was accused of masterminding the hit-and-run shooting of his former golfing partner in March the previous year. Prosecutors argued that he had planned the killing in an attempt to cover up his affair with Mr Zulkarnaen's third wife, a twenty-two-year-old caddie!

Reports suggested Mr Zulkarnaen was also blackmailing Mr Antasari over the affair, which could also have led to his murder. Tried with three fellow conspirators, he was sentenced to eighteen years in prison. Five other men, charged with carrying out the attack, were sentenced to seventeen or eighteen years in prison.

## THE GOLF BUZZ

Gary Player and Jack Nicklaus were attacked by a huge swarm of bees while playing an exhibition match at **Zwartkop** in South Africa in 1966. Covering their heads with towels, they made a run for it before wisely settling for a half on the hole. What they did not know is that African wild bees kill more people each year than any other form of wildlife!

RULE·VII·
A ball must
be played
wherever it
lies....